CULTURAL ETHOS
OF THE
YORUBA

Olubayọ Lawore

University Press PLC
Ibadan
2004

University Press PLC
IBADAN ABA ABUJA AJEGUNLE AKURE BENIN IKEJA ILORIN JOS KADUNA
KANO MAKURDI ONITSHA OWERRI WARRI ZARIA

ISBN 978 030 886 5

Printed by Kenbim Press Ltd. Ibadan.

Published by University Press PLC
Three Crowns Building , Jericho, P.M.B 5095, Ibadan, Nigeria
Fax: 02-2412056 E-mail: unipress@skannet.com
Website: universitypressplc.com

Contents

Dedication

I dedicate this book to the Yoruba people at home and in diaspora through the Elérùwá of Èruwà - the Ọba of a town well fortified by many hills, which includes Ọbasékú and Akolú rocks.

Acknowledgements

My thanks go to my friend, Kazeem Adejumobi (now of blessed memory), with whom I often had prior discussions before writing certain topics. I also thank my brother, Bolade Lawore, for his forthright corrections and I thank the Almighty God who supplied the inspiration and the will power.

Preface

Culture is more than dancing, display of works of art and staging cultural or even ritualistic plays and the films thereof. It does not end in traditional religious worship either. When a youth misbehaves and we blame him for lacking in culture we refer only to home training which he either does not have or he failed to imbibe. Nobody measures behaviour by the items of culture listed above and below.

There are many facets of culture. These include (1) art which is made up of drawing, modelling, crafts, carving, etc (2) aesthetic which is concerned with designs, patterns, sewing, dressing, etc. (3) religion (4) music in its various forms, types of instruments, methods of playing them and the sounds produced (5) dance - body movements and steps (6) "food - types..." and environmental influence (7) vogue which is concerned with art, aesthetics, music, dance, food, etc. Vogue is always transient, (8) behaviour which deals with acts and manners. The list is long. In summary, culture involves art, behaviour and religion.

This book is concerned only with the behavioural culture of the Yoruba people. Behavioural culture simply relates to how individuals do things, how they live and their inter-personal manners. But the Yoruba people have lost part of their behavioural culture to western civilization. This is evident in the way most youths and certain 'elitist elderly Yoruba' do things. The degree of the loss varies as to locality. For example, in the rural setting, the loss is either minimal or non-existent but in urban areas the loss is significant. If a Chinese, Indian or Japanese, for example, lives in the vicinity of the Big Ben in London or around the White House in Washington or even in an indigenous town like Ibadan, he will still maintain his tradition undiluted - no matter the number of years he is domiciled. But one cannot say the same of the Yoruba person. Thus, some Yoruba are more English than the English or more American than the Americans (not in language), even though they remain mere ridiculous imitators! To such Yoruba, since their home culture is different from that of the English or Americans it is 'backward'. This attitude is unhealthy. This is why social problems not known in our society in years past have today become threats to societal survival. Unfortunately, most 'been - tos' rather than come home with true 'civilization' have imported what can best be described as socio-cultural hybridity, which is tantamount to cultural pollution that breeds social chaos. Civilization is more of the correct application of modern technology to do things for better living. It is more scientific than cultural.

On the other hand, culture is truly dynamic but this affects the artistic aspect more than behaviour. To lose one's culture is to lose one's national identity and integrity. There is nothing like international or global identity as far as culture is concerned. You are either here or there or nowhere - just amorphous or anomalous! Even the UN does not attempt to fuse the culture of component members, hence the existence and acceptance of many languages *pari passu*.

I do not know of any people or race whose behavioural culture is comparable to that of the Yoruba. But it is sad to observe that many Yoruba people have become strangers in their own homes in an attempt to be what they can never be!

The time has come when the behavioural culture of the Yoruba should be taught and tested in schools. If this is done we would discover that if we place our culture along with any of the two universal religions, that is, Christianity and Islam, we would produce 'paradise' in our society to the benefit of all, thereby making our society a model for the world! The expression '*F'iwà k'ęsin*' (i.e. good character should be part of religion) suffices. Thus, religion devoid of good character breeds chaos and godless behaviour. You are implored to read this book for a proper comprehension and digestion of my position. It is a codification of what exists among the people with no personal addition or amendment. There are peculiarities in each of the many dialectal groups in the vast Yoruba race but what is treated in this book is common to all. The outlines of the subject matter discussed in this book are enough to know who the Yoruba people are.

Chapter 1

The Family

The bequest of colonialism as regards a family is father, mother and the child or children, this is the nuclear family. In the context of the Yoruba, a family is larger than that. The Yoruba person is his brother's keeper by tradition and this is why the extended family is the order of the day. The three-prong nuclear system is often regarded with scorn by neighbours who accuse the head of such a family as being selfish and miserly. It is common to see a family made up of the father, mother, children and a host of dependants, all under one breadwinner!

Dependants could be the parents of the couple, children of relations, the maid who accompanies the woman to her matrimonial home as ward, a stranger who sojourns in that community and chooses to live with the particular family, the wife of a brother who has travelled, or probably an apprentice. It does not however mean that all of those mentioned would be found in every family.

Sometimes, the parents of the couple do not live with them but whenever they do they are the responsibility of the couple who must cater for their welfare. Even up to this modern age, a man may decide to cater for the education of the children of some of his relatives because of some reasons. In some cases a childless couple takes on the upbringing of the children of other families. In such cases, except that the fostered child bears his real father's name in the school register, the people will call the child by the name of the man he lives with. If his own parents want to enquire about the foster parents, they will address them as the father or mother of the child who they did not raise biologically. Members of a childless family are always addressed by the name of children under their fosterage. They are happy to be so described. In Yoruba land, the childless are not really held with scorn but with a sort of disguised pity and love.

The people take the rearing of children as a blessing which must attend a marriage. In the past, the more children you reared the larger the size of your farm. They did not limit the number of children they could produce but sort

1

of planned their families. Thus, the gap between one child and the other was not less than two or three years.

In a family, there is no special treatment for any child or ward. That means if there is a maid in the family, she is treated like every other member of the family and the children will not see her as a stranger like we see in some modern families today. Therefore, the child and the maid receive the same quality of home training. At times, the children do not know that the maid is not born by their parents. In the case of a ward who has been employed for a specific duty, the mother ensures that the same volume of duty is performed by her own daughter and the ward.

When it comes to feeding, the whole family eats the same thing at the same time. If they are to be clothed, every member, apart from the couple and the elderly ones, will enjoy the facility. If the family is large and the parents cannot afford to buy clothes for them at the same time, this will be done by instalments till every member has got his own.

Courtship: In the Yoruba tradition it is the boy or his agent that woos a girl for marriage. The search for an intended wife (or future partner) used to be largely by proxy. The proxy method is in two forms. In the first type, it is the father that sees a young girl whom he wants to court for his son. Before arriving at the decision to court and marry her for his son, he must have, as a mature person, studied and approved the family of the young girl as one to be associated with. He would come home to tell his son of the 'jewel' and later arrange how the boy could go to the family to spy on the girl. He would then send his son on an errand to that family so that he could spy on his future wife. If he approves of the girl the parents of the boy would then visit those of the girl to announce their intention. After the consent of the girl's parents has been obtained, courtship begins. In some cases, the boy and the girl do not see face to face in the first three years - they only know they are future partners.

In the second proxy method of courtship, it is the boy that sees a girl of his choice and then hands the negotiation over to a close and trusted friend of his. In such an assignment the friend is doing the job of *alárenà*. Thus, *alárenà* is a go-between or intermediary between a boy and a girl in love. He is a marriage facilitator for the couple. It is he who brings the two partners together in love. During this period the family of the girl sees only the *alárenà* with their daughter whom they watch closely.

Visit: During a visit by the *alárenà* the girl escorts him to meet her future man who would be hiding some distance away. They are usually unable to look into each other's eyes because of shyness. The girl veils her face for the boy and they do not utter anything serious though inwardly both of them are joyous. In fact, any serious discussion they need to make must have been carried out earlier through the *alárenà*. If the girl wants anything from her boy she sends her own friend to the *alárenà*. This relationship continues till close to marriage.

Dowry: The English dowry is converse to that of Yoruba in that it is the boy's family that pays (in whatever form) to marry the girl. For example, in the olden days, the payment could be in the form of service - if the girl's father wanted to expand the acreage of his farm, he would send for the father of his prospective son in-law to inform him of it so that he would arrange a communal service whereby young men in their numbers would go and work on that farm. Apart from that, the boy would carry loads of food to the girl's parents annually. Firewood would also be taken there seasonally for the girl's mother. He would buy clothes for the girl to mark popular anniversaries. Gradually, the boy would equip the girl right from her parents' house. This practice might go on for several years. The reason is that courtship in those days began at a tender age when probably the girl had not reached puberty. Money (in cash) only came when they were about to be formally married. Such cash payment would however be minimal since the girl was not for sale. Even today, where modern courtship goes on many families do not emphasise cash while those who do so charge the barest amount.

The difference between the two proxy systems is that by the parent proxy the parents of the boy will directly study the home where the girl comes from to see if there are any social maladies or peculiar illnesses associated with them. And where there is none,the courtship goes on. In the friend proxy or *alárenà* the parents of the boy will carry out the investigation which the *alárenà* will not bother to do. It must be mentioned that the parents of the girl will also do a counter enquiry to ensure that their daughter is not going into a problematic home.

Today, the parent proxy has faded out as girls began to kick against parents giving them out like greeting cards to men they neither loved nor knew from Adam! In stemming this system, many girls who get married to old men absconded either before or a few days after the marriage. The system died a natural death even without anybody sitting down to plan how to stop it.

The friend proxy or *alárenà* has also been modified. This is because the Yoruba do not court infants as future wives any more. Young men and women, literate and non-literate meet and discuss marriage between each other, but in some cases, the *alárenà* still does the go-between.

Shy girls are better approached by the *alárenà* who operates both directly and through the girl's closest friend.

Similarly, love letters from boys usually contain interesting messages for their girlfriends. Added to this, occasional and seasonal cards also help to cement the love between both people.

It was customary among the Yoruba to consult the diviner, both the traditional seer and the prophet, to inquire into their prospective homes. Today, however, many youths are lackadaisical about this practice.

Marriage: Traditionally, marriage dates are arranged in two stages. The first stage is to arrange it to coincide with a particular season or an annual festival two to three years away. For the second stage, the girl's parents will fix a date of at least three months prior to the wedding. This tortuous dating is however no longer in vogue.

Two or three days to the wedding day, there will be celebrations in both families with lots to eat and drink. There will be music and dancing as part of the merry-making. In the night of the wedding, women, usually fairly elderly housewives from the groom's family will go to the bride's family to fetch her. There, the women with some men around will haggle a lot before actually being allowed to take the bride away. Housewives in the family house of the bride (or bride's agents) are the ones to demand cash, clothing, jewellery, etc as part of the final dowry from the bridegroom (groom's agents). The bride's agents will make impossible demands of things intended to be used by the bride while the groom's agents will prostrate, kneel and beg for consideration. Such demands as well as parental and family prayers could end around one or two o'clock in the morning. The bride's parents and other elderly members of the family will give their parental blessings and prayers to the bride before her departure.

At the bridegroom's house, more unreasonable and impossible demands will again be made by the bride's agents who escort her to her husband's house. One of the impossible demands by the new wife is that her husband should come out to meet her at the doorway before she can step into his house. By Yoruba tradition, the husband does not welcome his wife into his home. He is said to have travelled. He meets his wife in the room for the first time only at bed time after the retinue of escorts have departed. The second day, as the merriment continues, the husband will dance to his in-law's house in the company of his friends with a good society orchestra. This is a thank you visit.

Coup Marriage: In Yorubaland there is an unconventional type of marriage which is carried out by physically kidnapping the lady by agents of her would be husband. In the olden days when farming was prevalent they would lay ambush for her when she was either going to or returning home from her father's farm or while she was away from home for some reason.

This marriage form, though unconventional, is not less recognised. There are several reasons why people resort to *coup* or *capture* marriage. In most cases, if not in all cases, the man must have completed all the items of dowry due to the lady's family and to the lady herself. In other words, the lady must have been due for marriage or rather, over ripe for it. But here she is still looping in her mother's house when she is due to manage her own home!

There may be little wonder if she is kidnapped for marriage. One important point of note is that this *coup* marriage is never done without the prior knowledge of either the lady, the mother, the father or relatives, as the case may be. So, the act could depend on any of the following reasons:

(1)   If the mother shows too much affection for her daughter either because she is her pet or because of her usefulness to her and thus she has been delaying giving her out in marriage against the father's wish then the family of the husband could reach an agreement of *coup* marriage with the father to the surprise of the mother. Here the lady may not be aware prior to the act. In this case, close and distant family members and friends must have failed to convince the mother to accede to her daughter's marriage at different times.

(2)   Sometimes the delay comes from the girl herself. If she says she is unwilling the parents can not force her. In such a case, the father alone would have a prior knowledge of the *coup* but would never confess having approved of it so as not to annoy his wife.

(3)   But where the girl causes her own delay because she is *abàmi*, both father and mother would ask her would-be husband not to attempt any wedding ceremony but organise a *coup* marriage for her. Thus, they would assist the husband as to how they could overcome the negative traits in the girl without her knowledge. *Abàmi* refers to people who

5

either exhibit or hide some supernatural traits. Some are not conscious of their trait but many pretend ignorance.

One type of *abàmì* children are those called *emèrè*. These are children who are believed to live physically and also have continuous contact with the spirit world thus making them live in two worlds of earth and spirit. Not every parent can detect them in their negative, tricky form. Some parents who by accident discover them are helpless and keep the secret to themselves till the worst happens to such children. A girl in such a group could be in one of two categories. She may be the type that has vowed (from her spirit world) never to have an earthly husband. Many of them are around living well as single ladies. She may also be the type which wants to use the occasion of a grand wedding ceremony to bid farewell to earthly people and events so that any time between the marriage eve and child birth she could die and return to the spirit world. So when the father calls his would-be son in-law and plans a kidnap of the girl he knows what he is doing. Parents who are conscious of this are very few in any society.

This type of children are not necessarily *abìkú* (or *ogbanje* in Igbo) as very many people have wrongly held. The latter are products of either sickle cell or wrong blood combination between couples. *Emèrè* children are always beautiful or handsome, as the case may be, and are always successful in whatever they do while *abìkú* children are not always healthy. However some children combine the two.

(4) The young man himself may hate a formal wedding ceremony of any kind. He may even be the impatient type. He then surprises everybody in his in-law's household including his wife-to-be with a *coup* marriage.

(5) The news may leak of the intention of the girl to elope with another man. The *coup* system could be organised for her as quickly as possible.

Usually, after the girl has been either kidnapped, captured or *stolen* by her husband, she will normally weep. If she knows before hand she would only shed crocodile tears to deceive people but if she is unaware of the plan it remains a real *coup* to her. She will naturally feel very sad. Thus, she may hate the husband for two or three days while female relations, including her friends would stay near her and console her to accept the situation in which she finds herself.

At the other end, a powerful delegation from the husband excluding his parents, will be despatched to the girl's parents to either inform them of the kidnap if they had not known or plead with them to accept the situation. The delegation will shift the blame on the youthfulness or the impatience of the husband. They have no choice but to accept as they would be reminded that no parent ever marries his own daughter.

There is a modern form of *coup* marriage. The plan is hatched and executed between the lady and her suitor. In that case the length of courtship or the amount of dowry has no place but love. What happens is that the lady moves into the man's house. Immediately she gets there the two of them go to the nearest police station to report the voluntary *moving-in* of the lady. The purpose is to escape any criminal case of abduction against the man. It is normal today that cases of missing persons are reported to the police and if through the police swoop such a 'missing' girl is found in a man's house such a man will be in trouble. So, after reporting to the police, a message will be sent to the parents of the girl to inform them that their daughter has eloped with her husband. Even if the girl's parents were angry with the method, or with their daughter or her suitor, the news that she is alive would put their mind at rest. Subsequently, the relevant negotiations will now follow.

Virginity: Until recently, it was a pride for the bride, her husband and her mother for the lady to remain a virgin till marriage! The mother would be proud that her daughter kept her virginity. The household, made up of father, mother, distant relatives and close friends of the husband would all be on the watch to see if his wife was a virgin. This showed that the first lawful sexual contact was a sort of ceremony. If the husband indicated that his wife was a virgin, the two families and their neighbours would quietly rejoice and give great respect to the lady. In fact, it is on record that women who brought virginity to their husbands gained honour and respect in the community.

In a certain Yoruba community, the new wife would present a pigeon to her husband on her first day to indicate the absence of her virginity. The husband would use the blood of the bird to stain a white handkerchief purporting this to be the result of his breaking of his wife's virginity. It is this stained cloth he would display to indicate the *innocence* of his wife. This was aimed at covering the waywardness of the lady. Things are different today. People seem not to care any more for such things.

The Wife in the Family: By Yoruba custom, like other people, marriage of whatever type is sacred and so a wife is a sacred family member. Sacred in the sense that only her husband must have a sexual relationship with her. Should an extra marital sexual relationship occur in the traditional setting, the woman would be accosted and if she denies the charge, two steps would be taken against the Romeo man. Either they would hire thugs to beat him up, warning him never to conjugate the woman in question again or they would use *mágùn* to separate them. *Mágùn* is an occultic preparation projected secretly to a wayward woman so that any other man who has sex with her might contract a lethal feat. It is such that the man can be infested with several types of unsettled bodily conditions, which could lead to instant death if he does not find the antidote immediately. But if the woman with *mágùn* on her does not have sex with any man within, say, three days she could herself die unless the antidote is applied to her.

Where the woman is found to be promiscuous and she is involved in a scandal that brings shame to the family, she could be sent out of her matrimonial home. But she could be pardoned if she begs and promises to change from her waywardness.

In hierachy, the bride, being the latest addition to the family, is the lowest in the rung of the ladder of seniority. Thus, she is made the most junior in the family. This has nothing to do with age, but position. Any child born before her arrival into the family, be he an infant, is senior to her in rank. Everybody treats her so and she on her own gives due respect to everybody. This means two things to the new wife. First, anybody in the family can call her by her first name - though most people waive this to address her as *Ìyàwó* (wife). Second, anybody can send her on errand. This also is theoretical.

On her part however, the *Ìyàwó* can decide to do menial jobs for anybody within the larger family. When she does this, it is customary that anybody she so works for must give her some money either for doing the job or for merely attempting to do it. Most *Ìyàwós* used this method to collect money.

The minor responsibilities of an *Ìyàwó* include assisting family members in their chores i.e sweeping, carrying of loads, drawing water, pounding yam, washing dishes or clothes, etc. The doer would appreciate her attempt or willingness but would excuse her. She must not overlook any family member performing any form of task.

When a new wife is coming in, all the women in the larger family will use the occasion to extort money from her husband as if they are obtaining a sort of excise duty which allows the wife to live among them. It is a tradition which still goes on till today.

No woman is permitted by tradition to call her husband by his name. She says *Baálé mi* (my husband). When a woman starts to rear children, everybody including her husband begins to address her as *màmá Lágbájá*, usually the name of her first living child. *Lágbájá* is a pseudonym for anybody

8

you don't want to mention by name - man, woman or child, slave or free born.

The Wife and Names: In her matrimonial home, the new wife cannot call anybody by name, not even an infant, since they were born before her entry into the family. (Family in this sense is a larger one comprising either a compound or a village of various but united family units). Thus, she addresses every male youth as either *Oko mi* (my husband) - for those aged roughly between two and thirty years. Those aged up to sixty years are addressed as *Baba Oko mi* (father of my husband). Old people are simply *Baba* (father).

In the case of a female, those aged between two and fifty years are the mother of her husband *(Ìyá Oko mi or Yako mi)*. Old women are simply called *Ìyá* (mother).

Wives are fond of giving and addressing certain youths by their nicknames as a mark of respect. Sometimes, the nickname is a polite ridicule. For example, a short youth may be addressed as *a kúrú ye ijó* (one whose shortness is appropriate for him to dance beautifully well). On the other hand, the short youth could be called *Dóógó*. This is an adopted Hausa word meaning 'tall'. Sometimes the name becomes so popular with the person that people use it to address him to his own liking. This is how dwarfs are named *Dóógó* in Yoruba society.

If a young girl is naturally endowed with large buttocks she becomes *ìbàdí àrán,* meaning (the buttocks befitted with velvet). Velvet is a cloth covetted by everyone for making its wearer appear noble and regal. It predates lace and other costly material.

Similarly, an almost skinny lady or youth is given the nickname *awé-léwà,* meaning someone whose thinness makes her beautiful.

Wives often nickname infants with rotten teeth in two ways. First, as a direct ridicule, they are called *eyín aró,* (the teeth of indigo dye). The mothers of such children do not like it but merely tolerate the name but as the children grow older and wiser the nickname is changed to *eyín-afé,* (lovable teeth or teeth of love).

A very beautiful young girl is nicknamed *olójú egé* or *olójú ogc* (face of delicacy or beauty) while a male youth who always appears neat is addressed as *a jí gbó t'afé* or *a jí safé* (pleasure lover). The list is very long and it varies, sometimes from place to place.

9

Chapter 2

Greetings and Compliments

By tradition, the Yoruba people have different complimentary words of greetings for different occasions, situations and periods of the day and the year. This is probably because of their customary penchant to remain communicable to whoever is around them. It also borders on kindness, generosity and general love for fellow beings, irrespective of status and race. If you live with them and you speak their language and you are not in the habit of using greetings, they will challenge you strongly. If your language is different from theirs and you live among them, they, both young and old, male and female, will untiringly greet you as often as their custom permits.

This is why strangers who live among them often understand the language of greetings first and when they themselves want to learn another language, they start with the complimentary language. Another reason for this greeting habit borders on their great sense of socialization and brotherhood. Thus, for every action of man during all the minutes or seconds of the day, there is a language of compliment.

Morning and the Compliment Ambassador
In a traditional Yoruba setting where houses are built in circular compounds (this may not be peculiar to the Yoruba) the most elderly man and woman will wake up very early in the morning, possibly before others, to say 'Good morning' round all the houses and rooms, mentioning the names and praise names of the heads of every family and those of grown up children. The old man or woman, that is, the compliment ambassador, will in fact use the greetings to wake up those still sleeping, telling them the day has broken. Literally, the greetings go like this, as the old man only stands at the doorway because he has to reach many places: *Òjélàdé* or *John* (first name only of the head of the particular family). If there is no answer he will repeat once or twice and tap the door gently, calling again: *Òjélàdé.* If *Òjélàdé* is awake the old man then adds *Òjélàdé's* eulogy *Ìshòlá* or *Ìsòlá.* He then follows with *Kàárò ò. Ara ò le bí?* (Good morning. How is your health this morning? I

10

hope you are well?) He will quickly add a little part of *Òjélàdé's* family eulogy, *(Ìsòlá, omo aperin bí eni pa eliri. Jagunjagun t'ó pa egbèégbèrún láe làágùn. Dìde, Ilè ti mć (Ìshọlá,* the son of the hunter that kills lions like mouse rats? The warrior who killed thousands without sustaining any wound, etc. Wake up. The day is up). The old man will call the names and eulogies of everybody in that family, ranging from the oldest to the youngest. The old man goes round all the homes in his compound. He also goes to nearby compounds where he has relations. Yet he is back to his own home early enough for him to set out for his own daily duties, usually farming in those days, but later at the advent of colonialism trades like bricklaying, carpentary, etc. were introduced.

In fact this act is often performed by the head of the family. Women who carry the morning compliments around often fall into the category of the very old ones who have reached the age when the supporting stick forms their third leg.

Immediately each family wakes up or is woken up by the morning compliment ambassador it is now the turn of the head of the family or the father to first greet his wife and the children in turn, beginning with the oldest as he calls them by their names and their praise name only. The man does this either on his way to the bathroom to wash his face or as he lies on bed, depending on his schedule for the day.

After the man has done his part his wife takes her turn in greeting the household. She begins with her husband. In this modern era of polluted culture the woman would simply say -*Báále mi* or *Bàbá Kúnlé, káàrọ o* (My husband or the father of Kunle, good morning). This will be returned by the man who calls the woman by her praise name. But if it is the traditional setting which is still practised, the woman will actually, first say *Báálé mi, Olúwa mi, Olówó orí mi* (My husband, My lord, My total owner). She then kneels down in worship of her husband. She will follow this by saying 'Good morning' and before her husband returns the greetings she goes further to recite the man's family eulogy but she must not call her husband's *oríki àbísọ* which is only used by senior persons of the family. If the woman is a good practioner of tradition she would go further. From her kneeling position and while still eulogizing the man's family she would bend forward to touch the ground in turns with her left and her right shoulders as a sign of total submission to the authority of her husband. These acts will impel prayer from the husband and as he starts praying the wife, who is still kneeling, will remove her headtie or headgear with her head turned towards her husband, to 'wet' her head with the 'down pour' of prayers. After that she stands up saying *Mo dúpẹ́* (Thank you).

The husband's prayer is not recited the way a christian or moslem would say it. It is like this: *Àkànké, o káre. Wàá dàgbà, Wàá darúgbó. Oó jèré àwọn ọmọ rẹ. Ẹlẹ́dà bàbá mi kò ní ida àarin wa rú. Wàá kùtà sí ilé mi."* (You've done well, *Àkànké*. You will grow old in this house and be a prosperous mother of our children. God will look after our children. My father will not allow any circumstance to spoil our relationship. You will grow to be unmarketable in our family). This is another way of saying she will grow old and never be divorced or she will never have cause to be married to another man. The prayer will extend to the woman's daily ventures that she may prosper. At the end, the woman will stand up, say 'thank you' to the husband for all the prayers and then put on her headtie.

It is after this that the woman will compliment her children and/wards. Those greetings by the father and the mother to their children are primarily to wake them up. Now that the children are awake each of them must greet their parents. The males will prostrate while the females will kneel down to greet or worship their parents.

The family greetings pattern cited above is the standard one. There are additional ones and also variations depending on the dialectal groups.

Greeting Others

The Yoruba live by the extended family system. Where such families live near the home of the couple, the husband must visit them early every morning to greet them. Even the children must greet all the members of the larger family who may be living in adjoining rooms or house. One must greet anybody one sees or meets for the first time in the morning.

A youth who fails to greet an adult would be challenged for not doing so. Even when he meets strange adults on the way, he must exchange greetings with them. If he fails the adult may challenge him in any of the following - *Ìwọ kò mọ bí a tí nkí ènìyàn ni? O kò lcc kí mi káàrò ni? Ẹnu rẹ kò sẹ́ẹ́ kí ènìyàn ni? O mà ní àfòjúdi púpọ̀ o tí o kò mo káàrò wí.* (Don't you know how to greet? Can't you say good morning? Have you no mouth to greet? Why are you so insolent that you cannot say good morning? etc). After such a challenge, the youth would say, *Ẹ jọ̀wọ́, Ẹ ma bínú.* (I'm sorry, or Don't be annoyed with me). Then he greets accordingly.

Afternoon / Evening Greeting

Having treated greetings in the morning, we will discuss afternoon and evening greetings together. There are conditions under which one must say either good afternoon or good evening. If you are visiting somebody in his home, you will first say *Ẹ káàsán or Ẹ kú alẹ́, or Ẹ kú irọlẹ́* (Good afternoon or Good evening) Your host will return the greeting in the normal way. Your host will follow with *Sé dáadáa ni? Sé ko si nkan?* (How are you? or How are things?). He will later follow with an expression like *Sé kò sí láburú? Ò pẹ́ tí a ti rí ara wa!* (Hope nothing? or It's long we saw, hope there's nothing?). It is after such enquiries that the visitor says the object of his visit. If it is the host who invited the guest or if he is aware of the purpose of the visit he will not enquire why the visitor has come. He will simply say, (welcome, thank you) but only after the initial greetings initiated by the visitor. If you are a stranger and you are asking to be shown a place, your first compliment language is 'Good afternoon/evening/morning', depending on the time of the day.

Children in the family don't need to say Good afternoon/evening to their parents except when they are sent on an errand, where they must first say it to the person to whom they have to deliver the message as well as adults they meet on the way. However, children in the family say the afternoon- evening greetings only to adults visiting their home.

All-time Greeting

The Yoruba people greet each other for every action, every movement made in a day or every task performed. With the phrase beginning *Ẹ kú...* a person can be greeted one thousand times a day because their culture allows them to greet for whatever things he does throughout a day or a year.

Ẹ kú... has no equivalence in English language and there cannot be a literary translation of it but the idea could be conveyed as meaning 'Enjoy your..... or Do well ...' ('Do' is replaceable with the verb describing the particular action for which the one is being greeted). The *Ẹ kú...* greeting is a sort of encouragement and compliment. With that one will have the following for example: 'Enjoy your... (morning, afternoon, evening, sitting, dancing, load carrying, work, competition, merriment, sleep or sleeping, celebration, etc.'). Even for the seasons you could greet someone *Ẹ kú ẹ̀ẹ̀run /òjò/ oorun /òginninti /oyẹ́ /iri/ wẹli wẹli,* etc (Enjoy the dry season, winter, rainy season, sunny weather, cold weather, harmattan, dew, showers, etc.). That means you can greet your neighbour when he sits down, stands up, sleeps, is in crouching position, in prostration ,etc. The responses initially are the same, ie, *Òo,* A *dúpẹ́* (O.K, Thank you). You may add any other compliment

13

before going into serious conversation which you may have intended.

Let us examine some examples of the application of all time greetings.

(1) If you enter a public bus and you meet other passengers seated you will say to them generally: *E kú ijókòó* i.e (Enjoy your sitting, (**Note that in practice this English version is never used. It is literally here only to explain the Yoruba expression**). Then some or all of them will welcome you thus: *E káàbọ* or *káàbọ* (Welcome).

(2) If you have an agreement with one, two or three friends to meet ?t a place where you would board the same vehicle, the first person to arrive there has nobody to greet but others who arrive later will in turn say, *E kú iwájú* (Enjoy coming here earlier). As they return it with *'Oo* i.e (O.K) then you add, *E kú ijókòó o*, i.e (Enjoy sitting or your seat) to the person you are going to sit side by side with, who will also repeat *E kú àbò* (Welcome or Enjoy your coming).

(3) If it is a social gathering, you will first greet the early comers: *E kú iwájú o* i.e (Enjoy your early arrival or Enjoy your coming here before (me). Then you greet the person whom you will sit beside *E kú àsán / irọlé/alé* (Good afternoon or evening). When you sight the celebrant you greet him, *E kú ináwọ́* (Enjoy your spending). He will thank you.

(4) When you are going along the road you greet most of the people you meet *E káàbọ̀*, (Enjoy your coming or simply Welcome). Then both of you will say *o dabo* (Good bye) as you part in opposite directions. If someone is going in front of you and you have to overtake him you will say *E kú iwájú* (Enjoy being in front) before overtaking him. The overtaken person will respond: *E káàbọ̀, Ó dábọ* i. e (Welcome and Good bye). Then you will finally say as you pass him: *E máa kálọ* (Follow on). If as you go on the way and somebody is coming behind you and is fast enough to overtake you then you will greet him, *E máa kálọ* (Follow on). He will answer you *O o* (O.K) and as he passes, the greeting, exchange will be as the ones stated earlier.

(5) If you go to meet someone at his place of work you will greet him *E kú isẹ́* (Enjoy your work), to which he responds: *Oo káàbọ̀* (Thank you, welcome).

(6) When athletics or ball games are being played or people are just playing on, you will greet the participants or even the spectators: *E kú eré* (Enjoy your games). 'Thank you' is the appropriate answer.

(7) If it is a film or video viewing centre you have to greet them: *E kú iwòran* (Enjoy your viewing).

14

The general behaviour is that by custom the Yoruba first greet each other whenever they come together. The condition under which you meet will dictate the type of greeting. Thus, the first greeting may be any or the three time-of-day types of greeting as the case may be. The greeting type may as well be influenced by the action being performed by those being greeted. Thus, the 'Enjoy ...' pattern could be more appropriate.

Please, note that in English 'Good evening' covers dusk to sundown to late night but the Yoruba split the period into three:

(i)   *Ẹ kú irọlẹ́* (for after dusk)
(ii)   *Ẹ kú àsáálẹ́* (for dusk period only)
(iii) *Ẹ kú alẹ́* or *Ẹ káalẹ́* (for sundown or nightfall till late night).
       Similarly for the morning time:
(i)   *Ẹ kú idájí* (for the dark period of the morning)
(ii)   *Ẹ kú kùtùkùtù yií* (for morning twilight)
(iii) *Ẹ kú àárọ̀* (for daylight morning)
       Greetings in Yoruba are inexhaustible.

Individual-Group Contact
When a person comes in contact with a group or crowd of people, it is only in two cases that the group will first greet the individual. It is in the situation where a teacher meets his students or when the king or a ruler is in contact with a group of subjects. In such cases the students greet according to any of the three time-of-day greetings or they simply say 'Welcome'. It depends on the situation. In the case of the appearance of the king or ruler, the group or crowd will echo *kábíyèsí* (Your majesty). Traditionally, the royal personage will not reply by himself but will only shake his tassel which is a beautiful, white horse tail. As the royal tassel is raised a senior court official will immediately speak for him saying: *Ọba ń kí yín* (The Ọba greets you, the oba wishes you well). The same type of greeting is used for the nation's president, prime minister and a governor, who should be simply accorded 'Welcome'

Apart from these two conditions, it is the individual who must first greet when in contact with a group of people.

Welcome
The use of 'welcome' is not as it is in English. English usage where its application has a tincture of royalty for occasions coloured with pomp and pageantry. The Yoruba apply it in quite a different sense. It will be unfair to

ascribe banality to its Yoruba application simply because one can use it a thousand times within a day. It is *Ẹ kú àbọ̀* or *Ẹ káàbọ̀*.

First to Greet

There is the element of who should be first to greet in Yoruba culture. This continues to cause controversy among peers and colleagues. For example, if an elderly person and a youth meet, and the two of them are conscious of the time they met, it is the junior person that must first greet the adult. But if they met and only one of them, be it the senior or junior, was aware of the presence of the other, it is the one that is aware of their meeting that should greet first.

Even where two friends meet, the latter principle is applicable. But if they meet suddenly they unconsciously greet one another simultaneously and exchange more compliments in their familiar, friendly way. Usually a hysteric barrage of greetings with hugging or joining of hands may follow when they suddenly meet.

Except in the case of compliment ambassadors, it is the junior that must first greet an elderly person. The wife also must first greet the husband in the morning. Even when the husband that wakes her up with the morning compliments, the wife will on waking up formally greet her husband, with 'Good morning'. If it is a situation of master and servant, the servant must greet first. In the case of a visitor, be he a stranger or a friend, he cannot freely move round the home of his host and so, no matter what his age, the host must first greet the visitor in the morning.

Negative Compliment

There is no human action or occurrence that does not attract its own form of greetings by Yoruba practice. As a background, the word GREET is used for the purpose of compliment as well as to express sympathy and so the actual Yoruba word is *'Kí'*, meaning to greet or to sympathise. The frequency at which complimentary greetings are applied daily almost equals that of sympathy expressions.

If you sneeze the people around you will say 'sorry' (*pẹlẹ* or *ẹ pẹlẹ*) instead of you to beg for pardon. If it is an adult or an important person who sneezes everybody around will bid him 'sorry'; some will chorus it, others may prefer saying it individually, but the purpose is to let you know they love you. The same thing happens when you cough in public. It is the people around you that will greet you with 'sorry' and not you begging anybody for pardon. If it is royalty who sneezes or coughs nobody will say sorry as they do to other people but it is compliments galore, 'Your majesty', 'Your Highness', that is *Kábíyèsí*.

If you walk along the road and you knock your foot against an obstacle people around you - will say 'Sorry'(*pèlé* or *e pèlé*). While some other cultures may see such as an act of carelessness, the Yoruba people feel for the pains you may suffer. They will ask you whether you are hurt (*se ko bu?*) and even the degree of the wound you sustained. Since the people often went about bare-footed in those days (the weather permitted this) they got some bad wounds at times whenever they knocked their feet against obstacles.

Sorry

The English expression of the word is widely used by the Yoruba elite but not always in the sense of English usage. The use of the word may sometimes be inappropriate by English usage yet only approximate for the sense it is applied in Yoruba. This is because it is a translation of *E pèlé* or *pèlé* which though is usually taken to be 'sorry' can literally be taken care of by simply saying either 'Gently' or 'Go gently' or 'Act gently' or 'Be careful' or even 'Be comforted'. Thus *pèlé* or *E pèlé* is the general expression yet in semantics the objects for expressing it vary in degree according to seriousness and situation . Yoruba people comfort somebody in sorrow or pain. *Pele* in full is *Se pèlépèlé, E pèlé* in full is *E se pèlépèlé*. It all means 'Be careful' *E* is the plural used to address
(i) a senior (ii) nobility (iii) more than one person.

Compliment in Arrears

The cultural make-up of the Yoruba seems to dub them as a race that has time for pleasure like all tropical Africans. That is wrong. However, no matter how busy one may be or even how difficult the task at hand is one is expected to accord compliments when they are necessary. This is a culturally in-built behaviour. Thus compliments in arrears come either at the end of a day or after an event has taken place. For example, when someone holds a party and his guests see him for the first time after the event they will greet him with *E kú ináwó àná, òsè tí ó kójá, ojó sí. Olúwa yòò bo àsiri.* (thanks for the party of yesterday or last week, Enjoy your spending, May you not be over burdened by the expenses). He may add a further complimentary sentence: *Mo gbádùn ináwó náà,* or *ináwó yín náà gà púpò* (I (we) enjoyed the party very much). Another race may simply say 'Thanks for the party.'

The host must respond to the compliment by saying: *E sée, Mo dúpé o, rcrc ni a ó máa bá ara wa sc o, c kú àdúró tì mi o,* (Thank you, may we have occasions of joy to celebrate together, I enjoyed your company).

It is not the host alone who expresses post-party compliments. The parents or parents-in-law (as the case may be) will also go through the compliment course. Similarly, elderly persons living nearby who did not attend the party will come to the host's house the following day to congratulate him on the success of the gathering.

The practice is that some food is sent round the homes of neighbours who might not have been present at the party. This is to give such people a taste of the party. Yet, all of them thereafter would come to the host to express their post-party compliments.

If the party was a flop through lack of attendance most of the perishable items would end up in the dustbin. Sympathisers would greet the host / victim: *E pèlé o* (sorry). They would advise him: *Nse ni kí e ta àwọn ohun tí kò lè bàjé,* (You better sell the non-perishable things). If the flop was caused by hoodlums resulting in serious damage to property, sympathisers would greet him: *E pèlé,* (Sorry), *Olúwa yóò fi òfò ra èmí o,* (May the Lord recoup your loses with gifts of life). His responses: *Mo dúpé, e sée o, irú èyí kò ní selè sí òdò yín o,* (Thank you, may you not experience such happenings).

Party Greetings

While the party is going on the air is usually rife with a kind of market place noises of familiar, friendly discussions and compliments, apart from the sound of music, if there is any. This may not be peculiar to the Yoruba. As the guests trickle in they will first look for their host to say, *E kú ináwó. Àsírí yóò bò o.* (Enjoy your spending, May you not be over burdened by the expenses). The host will welcome them, thank them and offer them seats.

The guests themselves will exchange greetings lavishly because there is time for that, that is, the party time! They may greet each other thus: *E káàbọ, E kú àbase, A ó máa rí rere bá ara wa se o* (Welcome, Enjoy your participation, May we always have cause to enjoy good things together) Of course, 'Amen' and 'Thank you' are the answers.

Then as the party goes on the host either with or without his wife will go round to greet the guests. A female host would perform her 'thank you' greetings as she goes round several times saying, for example, *E kú ikàlè, E kú à-bá se, Mo dúpé, A ó máà rí rere bá ara wa se o,* (Enjoy your sitting, enjoy your participation, Thank you, May we continue to have cause for joyous celebrations together. 'Enjoy the night /day /dawn'. The guests will return the greetings.

18

Appropriate greetings accompany each category of social party but 'well spending' or 'Thanks for spending' or 'Thanks for the expenses' are common to all.

The following are appropriate compliments for each category of party in addition to those treated above.

Category	Guest's Compliment	Host's Response
1. Child naming	*Kí Olúwa dá ọmọ náà sí* (May God spare the child)	*Kí Olúwa wò wón pò* (May God spare all of them). *Olúwa yóò pèsè ọmọ fún ẹyin náà o.* (May God provide yours to an adult that has not got a child).
2. Birthday	*Ìwọ yóò se ọpọ ọdún láyé o.* (May you celebrate very many more years of life).	*Mo dúpé o* (Thank you)
3. Marriage	*Ọmọ nísìsìyí o* (May children come in soonest).	*A dúpé o* (Thank you)
4. Burial and Bereavement	*Ẹ kú à-sèyin-dè* (Sorry for the death) *Òkú yóò yamọ o,* (May the dead replicate himself)	*Ojó yóò jìnà sí ara wọn* (May death dates be distant. i.e to live long after the deceased)
5. Graduation	*Yóò rí isé rere se o* (May he/she (graduant) secure good job). *Yóò lo irin-isé jèrè o* (May he use his tool profitably).	*Rere á kárí o* (May good things go round).

Note that compliments regarding spending as well as gratitude and other basic ones already mentioned are omitted in the table above.

Some Other Greetings

1. **Pregnant woman** - greet her *Àṣòkalè aǹfààní o*, (safe delivery). Greet her husband or her mother or aunt - *A ò gbóhùn iyá a ó gbóhùn ọmọ o*, (May we hear the child cry and the mother talk).

2. **The invalid**- greet him, *Olúwa yóò mú àlàáfià wá*, (May you regain your good health May God give you good health).

3. **Bereavement** - greet the bereaved, *Olúwa yóò dáwọ́ rè dúró o* (May God terminate/stop untimely deaths). He then responds *A kò níi fi irú èyí san án fún ara wa, Ọjọ́ á jin sí ara wọn o* (May we not repay death with death. May death's dates be distant).

Chapter 3

Respect

The Yoruba attach great importance to respect in the same way they give prominence to greetings and compliments. Respect is one of the important pillars upon which good manners rest in the Yoruba culture. It is an important behavioural culture otherwise called home training.

In Language

The first aspect of respect to be treated falls under the use of language. Like the French who have *tu* and *vous* to mean 'you' in singular and familiar way and 'you' in the plural and respect form respectively, the Yoruba also have *iwo* and *èyin* or 'o' and 'ẹ' to mean 'you' in singular or familiar and in plural forms. Thus the 'banal you' (*Ìwọ* or O) is applied by an elderly person to a youth. Example: *Ìwọ ni mo fẹ́ rí,* That is, 'It is you I want to see'. Also, *Njẹ́ o rí mi?* i.e. 'Did you see me?' Conversely, if a youth should speak the same sentence to an adult he will say, *Ẹ̀yin ni mo fẹ́ rí* and *Njẹ́ ẹ rí mi?* respectively.

Elderly persons and rulers make use of the 'banal you' or 'you' in the singular form more often than other individuals because of their socio-cultural position. What 'banal you' means here is the familiar way two friends or two youths, for example, address one another. People who are older in age or higher in status are addressed by others with the plural 'you'. So, in daily life every younger person (of whatever age) must address all older persons in the plural or the respect 'you'. So it is for all juniors (in status).

The respect 'you', is also applied by everybody (of whatever age) to rulers, society heads, bosses and academic seniors.

Despite the foregoing, there are categories of elderly persons and people in positions of authority who apply a special 'you' to address others with respect. The word is *ÌRẸ*. Its use however is diminishing quickly in the elitist society. It is usually applied to respectable, younger persons, especially by those of the same age or within the same age bracket but who each command respect in commerce, industry, politics, religion, etc. We have been treating

21

the application of the forms of 'you' (i.e. *Ìwọ- ẹ̀yin; o-ẹ* and *Ìrẹ*) in the use of language to promote respect. The next is the use of he/she (*oun* and *o)* and they (*àwọn* and *wọn)*. That is, *oun* and *'o'* mean HE/SHE while *àwọn* and *wọn* stand for THEY . So, the calibre of person who deserves the plural 'you' that is, *eǹyin* is he who gets the honour in the respect 'they' known as *àwọn*. Thus, the pronoun is applied by the Yoruba both to denote its plural form and also to respect an individual for his or her age or position.

The purpose of the above is not to teach the grammar of the language but to show that the Yoruba language gives room for the etiquette of seniority and respectability in addressing individuals whose positions or status demand such.

In Greetings

Greeting has been treated in chapter one. So the treatment here is different. The tradition is that the junior must first greet the senior at a conscious encounter. Thus, the child must first greet his parents. In the case of two friends or equals, it is the one who first sees the other that must greet first to establish a communication between them at that point in time.

Greeting can be in any language whatsoever. The most important thing is the act that goes with it. It is a salute but not in the military way. In Yoruba tradition, the junior male must prostrate or bend for the elderly person. That is, if the elderly person is much older, the junior must prostrate completely but where one is only slightly older the junior one will bend. In this case, the junior bends to a state which almost makes him touch the ground with his right hand. Otherwise he (the junior) just gives a slight forward jerk of the body - not a nod. As for the junior female, she must kneel for a very elderly person but for someone who is slightly older she can make a bend jerk similar to that of the male.

The respect situations treated above are applicable under the following conditions:

1. During morning greetings in the family and last thing at night before going to bed;
2. Any time of the day when the two persons first come in contact. This may be at a social gathering or a casual meeting; and
3. Whenever the junior offends the other party like mistakenly stepping upon his toes or causes any form of inconvenience, or unknowingly uses offensive language against him. In such situations the one that caused the offence must first be sorry for his action. Thus, remorse is an act of

respect. In expressing remorse, the offender will say *Jọ̀wọ́* or *jọ́ọ́* or *E jọ̀wọ́ or E jọ́ọ́* which means 'please' (by English expression it should be 'sorry') to an elderly person while to an equal or one slightly older he will in addition say *Ẹ má bínú* (Don't be annoyed). A third person who is friendly to the offender will add his voice to the expression of remorse to the aggrieved by saying *Ẹ dákun, ẹ má bínú* (Please don't be annoyed).

In Task Performance
The Yoruba people exhibit respect in the performance of various tasks. The bulk of this probably is in the family. There are two categories of human beings who carry out domestic duties in the family. These are the children and the wives. In the case of the young ones it is they who are called upon to sweep and wash dishes in the morning. Female youths warm the family soup in the morning and draw water for domestic use. The youths generally run minor errands like buying cigarettes, kolanut or, inviting neighbours for discussion or just taking messages to neighbours and similar small tasks. If there is a baby in the family it is the youths who sit with it while the mother is busy with domestic chores or has to be away from the family home for some reason. This task can be performed by either the male or female youths. However, the female youth has the cultural responsibility of sheathing the baby at her back if continuous sitting is causing strains. When the mother is busy with domestic chores the less busy children must stand-by for contingent errands, even though this serves as a sort of tutelage for the youths to learn from the mother how to do domestic tasks.

Elder-Youth Relationship
In the totality of human behavioural pattern the elderly person, that is, somebody who is older than the other by at least five years or thereabouts, has a natural superiority over the junior one. It is morally wrong to be rude to an elderly person for any reason whatsoever. Even if the elderly person is at fault; (and this supersedes Yoruba tradition), the junior one must accord him the required respect (even if grudgingly) because nature (or succinctly, God) is always behind the elderly person.

Thus, if a junior person insults an elderly person either for the fun of it or for some perceived wrongdoing by the latter, whether or not the offending youth is punished he has placed a curse on himself. So his punishment could be in any form either in the near or distant future. Only nature can determine what and when the punishment can occur.

23

If the elderly person actually behaves stupidly or unreasonably before the young person insults him, as a counter reaction, the latter would yet not go unpunished by nature. What will happen is that a situation of contributory negligence would exist between them whereby both of them get punished at whatever degree nature may decide and at whatever unspecified time, and the form of punishment cannot be determined by any human being. But it will surely come.

The lesson in the latter situation is that the youth is supposed to tolerate the insults or foolishness of the older person as a mark of good culture or proper home training. In cases where he endures the older person's misbehaviour nature will definitely compensate him (now or in future).

The lack of such tolerance on the part of the youth of today contributes to the perverse and decadent nature of the society.

As for the erring elder, nature or God knows what makes him 'tick'. Only nature knows whether that elderly person deserves to be punished for the misdeed or not. For example, at the time of misdeed he may have an unbearable psychological problem. He could be fatigued. He could be senile or absent-minded. He could be a habitual bully, or he could be naturally fretful or irritable. Because some of such behaviours verge on madness, especially in public, it is not for the young person to even comment on that or mock him, so as not to incur the wrath of nature.

The statement in Yoruba: *Ìwà àgbààyà l'ẹ hù yan* is very grave. That is, 'You have behaved like a foolish elderly person'. It MUST never come out of the mouth of a tutored youth for any reason whatsoever. Such language upsets an elderly person whether he is at fault or not. A youth should not in anyway taunt an elderly person. He is supposed to treat the elderly with tenderness, respect and tolerance.

In practice, if other elderly persons were around when the misbehaviours mentioned above were committed by either of the parties, they would adjudicate the case in their wisdom. They would let the youth know that he should put the elderly person in the place of any of his parents or elder brothers or sisters whom he would naturally revere, while they would also blame the older person for his wrongdoing and advise him against wanton acts in future.

In the elder-youth relationship, the youth is placed in the orbit of the natural law of retribution. Thus, he would some day in future have somebody do to him exactly what he did to an elderly person. No prayer nor sacrifice can avert retributive justice. For it to come positively is for one to act rightly when the situation knocks.

24

On a last note, the elder-youth relationship is beyond human rights rule. Nobody can query nature.

It is an axiom that the youth will some day become elderly, if he lives. And may he live. Amen.

At Dinner

There are two ways of observing dinner by the Yoruba. It is either the whole family sits together to eat from the same plate, if the family is not large, or if it is large, two groups will emerge. For example, in a family with just two or three children, either with or without a ward or maid, all of them will eat from one plate as the father, mother and the children sit round their dinner.

As a mark of respect, the father must be allowed to be the first to cut his own morsel out of the heap of cassava mash (ẹ̀bà or àmàlà) or pounded yam, followed immediately by the mother and then the children. Thereafter, the children have no more restrictions even though there may be one or two who are fast eaters. At the end of the meal the youngest child will throw away the water used for washing hands clearing and washing of the plates is shared by the others. The mother assists in rolling up and removing the mat on which the kids sat i.e. if the others are all busy, otherwise, one of them will be directed to do that. Even before eating, preparations entailing mat spreading and getting water ready are the responsibilities of the children. Some of these tasks are rostered so as to avoid the usual buck passing by the children who in the process often grow boisterous and quarrelsome.

Between Husband and Wife

Culturally, the wife is junior in rank to the husband even if she is actually older. She respects her man by performing all tasks that fall within her responsibilities. These include food preparation both in the kitchen and at the table as well as child caring. She does not however run errands for her husband in the same way as the children would do. The husband also shows respect for his wife by assisting her if the task on her hand is crippling. For example, if they are walking along and the wife is carrying the baby on her back with a load on her head, the husband would assist her if he notices that the child is giving her some problem. But as soon as the child stops its disturbance the woman would, out of respect, take the load from her husband. The husband may or may not return it. If they are going to the farm and the husband needs to carry a basket or calabash it is the woman who will carry it for him. Therefore, as a way of commanding respect the husband does practically nothing at home except minor tasks at his wife's request.

25

Between Two Friends

As mutual respect is one of the ingredients of love, two people cannot claim to be friends if they do not respect one another. Two friends do not need to formally allot tasks to one another in the face of the many jobs that need to be done. Each of them would willingly pick any of the tasks, usually the toughest or the most delicate one. So, the keypoint here is that a friend shows respect to his friend in task performance by voluntarily struggling or wishing to do a greater volume of the work or face the most demanding situation. In fact, the degree of respect between two friends is dictated by the type of relationship that exists between them. For example, the relationship between two male friends is often communal, whereby either party makes some personal sacrifice to their union. This explains why men's friendship is in most cases tight and lasting, unlike the female, whose friendship by nature is delicate, fragile and sometimes fraught with mutual suspicion.

The In-law

In-lawship has two sides: male and female. The male side are the relations of the huband while the female side are those of the wife. By Yoruba tradition, the female side is 'senior' to the male side because it is the male that cringes to gain possession of the wife from the female side. Therefore, ordinarily the female side commands the respect of the other side. The same thing goes for task performance. When any member of the female side (father, mother, brother, sister, etc.) visits the male side, the treatment is always mini-royal. The visitor is accorded special attention with the whole household serving him or her, irrespective of the age. Incidentally, the same thing happens if it is a member of the male side who visits the female. What affects this situation apart from in-lawship is the traditional treatment of visitors with respectful courtesy. Where in-laws of the two sides meet at a neutral ground, usually informally, the normal respect of the female side prevails, even in task performance.

In such a situation it is common to have the youths of both sides coming together in good friendship thereby cancelling the delicate thread of in-lawship. Thus, how they respect each other and how tasks are performed depend on either age or the degree of friendship.

Visitor or Stranger

As briefly mentioned in the last topic, a visitor or a stranger is treated in a kingly (or queenly) fashion by his host. The same regard is accorded to him in task performance except that he feeds, baths, clothes and moves about himself like any normal person. Usually, guests either - strange or known-are regarded as people in transit, who deserve royal treatment.

Teacher / Pupil / Parent

The respect which the teacher commands among pupils or students varies from that of the parents. Previously the respect for the teacher by students was based on fear. The teacher used to cane at will as a result of which no pupil would even like to come face to face with him anywhere not even outside the classroom. But to the parent, the teacher conjures respect because of the selfless nature of his service in educating the children. Thus, anything needed or demanded by the teacher from the parent is promptly provided. At the village setting the teacher used to be the centre of attraction for his exposure and exemplary life style. Today, things have changed. The teacher still enjoys the people's respect but it is no longer as it used to be.

Name Calling

The junior one must not call anybody older than him by his name. Once somebody is older than you, you are permitted only to address him as 'brother', 'sister', 'father' or 'mother'. These are mere pseudonyms! It does not matter whether you are related or not. The above pseudonyms do not have the usual English meaning but are meant to contrast the age of the junior from that of the senior. If he is as old as your elder sister, brother, father, etc. then he should be addressed as if he is your elder sibling and biological father. If there is a blood relationship, the junior will address the senior as *Ègbón mi* but if they are not related he would simply say *Ègbón* - 'my senior' and 'senior' respectively.

As a junior officer in working situations you address your senior as 'Master' if he is non-Yoruba, otherwise you call him *Ògá* meaning 'Master'. Actually, *Ògá* is always used in offices since the word 'master' denotes some servant-master relationship.

The foregoing treatise of RESPECT is the standard. But there will always be violators of every good intention, plan, practice and policy of man, hence, the establishment of the police and law courts. Consequently, there are problems millititating against respect in this era. The ever growing population in our urban cities is infested with cultural hybridity which some may call

27

cultural dynamism but the practice of which is detrimental to the moralising Yoruba culture. As part of this, most Yoruba families who are living in urban centres rather expend great efforts to ensure that their children always speak the English language more than their native language. Similarly because of the ever present rat race many parents concentrate more on family welfare than any aspect of culture. This is cultural decay! Yet many Yoruba persons in the diaspora are assiduously guarding the Yoruba culture, despite their exposure! That is the platform today–hence the need for this book!

Chapter 4

Table Manners

Ọba l'oúnjẹ (eating is royal). This is a Yoruba expression meaning that meal times should be respected by everybody - the person eating, regardless of age or status should not be troubled in any way till he has finished with the meal. The meal of an average Yoruba family is hot in terms of the spice content. In fact, there is no soup prepared without pepper the small pepper being preferred because it is the hottest. The reason why the Yoruba like hot taste lies in the fact that they believe that hot food clears the brain of debilitating mucus and makes the stomach settle rightly. Consequently, it is common to see people clearing their throat and nose during and immediately after a meal while they are also blessed with post-digestion free bowels. In fact, a meal with pepper soup constantly gives good health - the hotness must be tolerable however. The result is agility. No wonder the Yoruba have a saying that *Ẹ̀mí tí kò jẹ ata ẹ̀mí yẹpẹrẹ ni* (the soul that is not fed with pepper is a weakling) to show how important it is to them is to eat food served with soup well savoured with pepper.

Food
It is necessary to consider what constitutes food in the Yoruba context. Their food or main meal is made up of two things - the paste and the soup. The paste could be made from either cassava, yam, cocoyam or plantain. It could also be a mixture of cassava with yam, cocoyam with yam or plantain with yam. If the tuber or the plantain is dried the paste is called *àmàlà* but if it is turned or pounded in cooked form the product is *iyán* i.e. pounded yam. When it is treated from its fresh state, especially cassava, the result is *fùfú*. See the table overleaf:

Sources and Types of Yoruba Food Pastes

Tuber	Sun-dried	Cooked	Fresh
1. cassava	àmàlà(white)	iyán	fùfù
2. yam	àmàlà (brown)	iyán	òjòjò cake
3. cocoyam	àmàlà (brown)	iyán	òjòjò cake
4. plantain (fruit)	àmàlà (greyish)	iyán	-
5. Mixture: of 2 + 1, 2 + 3, 2 + 4	àmàlà	iyán	-

The paste is eaten in morsels which are cut with the hand according to the swallowing capacity of the individual.

The second thing making up a major food or meal is the soup which is often in two parts - the vegetable and the pepper soup. The former is either purely vegetable or vegetable with melon. The latter contains either meat or fish. The two are mixed to form the soup which is eaten with the paste even though they are cooked separately.

The vegetable soup being discussed is the one cooked with little or no pepper and with or without ground melon. It is called pepper soup because the water used for boiling the meat or fish is mixed with a considerable amount of ground pepper to make it hot, according to the taste of the family or individual.

The treatment of food here is inexhaustable.

Talking

Because of the reasons given already the people probably rule against talking during meals. For the young ones it is a rule that must not be broken. They are compelled to maintain absolute concentration while eating.

Let us now examine some of the negative effects of talking while eating. One: The period of eating will be prolonged. Two: There is the possiblity of someone choking. Choking which is induced by food prepared with African pepper is deadly as the victim suffers greatly from the pangs of choking.

Lastly, it is hardly possible for anybody to talk while eating a meal of peppered soup without sending splutters to the faces of the others who are eating with him and to the meal itself. So, if one considers the side effects of talking while eating one would not quarrel with any restriction placed on it for children. The same goes for singing; nobody sings while eating.

Rushing and Stooping

By nature children like to rush through everything they do just as they prefer to run rather than walk. Rushing food often takes along the acts of loud and irregular breathing. Consequently, one feels there are gaps in the stomach within swallowed morsels. This results in drinking of water to press down the swallowed morsels and is often followed by belching to the disgust of others. Rushing of food can also cause choking when swallowing of the food does not synchronize with normal breathing. Stooping can easily cause choking and this is why parents always warn children against it while eating, so that food (i.e. oil particles or droplets from the peppered soup) might not rush out via the nose. This is common under situations of restlessness or tension caused by the hurried finishing of an assignment or sport, with the intention of resuming action immediately after.

Eating and Drinking Noisily

These are faults usually found in children. They stem from their love for play - they would want to eat fast to catch up with peers at play. Sometimes it may be that a particular child is trying to cultivate the habit of carelessness. The parents will always check his noisy eating or drinking habit till he gets rid of it. Drinking in a bubbling, whistling or trumpeting manner is a very bad habit. Noisy eating or drinking does not necessarily result in choking (this does not mean it cannot) but it causes unsettled stomach as a result of trapped air which will later try to escape through the mouth (via belching) or the anus thus defiling the air on each occasion of such gaseous release.

Water Drinking

Young children are prohibited from drinking water within meals unless the soup is very hot in taste. However, there are some children whose tastes are offended by the degree of hotness of the soup. When parents observe how such children are troubled by the burning effect of the pepper, they are allowed to drink a minimun quantity of water while still eating.

Parents try as much as possible to prevent their children from drinking water while eating for two important reasons. The first reason is that a child who drinks water often during a meal will have quicker digestion because he has

31

taken more water than food and as such will worry the mother for more food before the next meal is due. The parent may have to look for something to sustain him until the next meal is ready. This is not the case with the other child who drinks water only after the meal. The second reason is the prevention of bedwetting by children. Yoruba people frown at an older child who is still wetting the bed. He is disgraced on every occasion. Nobody sympathises with him. In the past during moonlight time other children would make jest of him. They also sang folk songs to satirise him. In the olden days such a child, if he was a school pupil, would be reported to the teacher and he would find himself within a circle of fellow students who would compel him to dance to their songs of mockery and humiliation. These are some of the reasons why parents prevent their children from drinking too much water with their meals especially during supper.

Errands
Parents do not send their children on errands during meal times, no matter what happens. They also prevent anybody from sending them on errands for the same reason. And once those who send such children on errands discover that they are having their meal the message will have to wait till after meal time. The implications of any such errands have been treated already. But, this rule is also broken mildly when it is discovered that there is not enough salt in the soup, for example. It is one of the children who will fetch it. This is safer because of the very short distance. If by accident, the drinking water finishes or is mistakenly spilled one of the children would have to temporarily stop eating to replace it. Even if the stew finishes the eldest of the children has to replenish it.

Near Side of Plate
Members of a Yoruba family traditionally sit round the meal. Customarily, they all sit round a heap of food mash and soup. While eating under this arrangement it is the practice that everybody cuts morsels from his side of the plate and dips them in the soup at the same point. Thus, anyone who stretches his hand to a side other than his could cause collision of hands over the food and that is an intolerable nuisance. It is an indecent act. If a child at meal sees a small piece of meat at the far side of the plate and wants to dip his morsels there in order to pick it, he may receive a hard knock on his head to teach him a lesson to never again encroach on other people's territory on the food plate.

Neatness at Meals

Before a child is allowed to eat away from home he must have become perfect or nearly so in table manners. For example, if he is to be seen as being decent at meal times he must cut his morsel in such a way that the food does not scatter or that crumbs fall here and there. He must dip his morsel neatly in the soup without allowing soup oil to spill on anything - be it on the plate edge, the ground or other people's hands or even on himself. It does not matter if the soup is the drawing type like okro. No spillage is allowed. His own fingers must not be smeared with the mash but should shine with the oil from the soup which will aid a neat cut of the paste. It takes extra care for one not to smear one's clothes with oil from soup, yet, the child is strictly watched by the parents against this. Any infringement earns him a knock on the head or a harsh reproach.

It should however be noted that an infant is too young to observe these rules by himself. But he is trained daily to eat by himself without anybody feeding him (with morsel food).

Meat

Meat forms part of a morsel meal except with vegetable soup which the village man or traditional Yoruba man regards as an alternative to meat because one has to first chew it before swallowing it with the morsel. After the meat has been shared among the meal participants, adults can eat theirs at will but the young ones are instructed not to eat theirs till after the meal. This is done for some reasons. With soft meat, he would quickly consume his portion only to look at his mother for more. If the meat is not soft, two things could happen. The child would want to eat it at all costs and in the process spill oil on his clothes and eyes and on the people near him. Again, in an attempt to eat it he could pay more attention to it than the food, thereby spending more time on the meal.

Parents cannot tolerate any of these acts, and that is why they rule children out of eating their meat during the meal.

Washing of the hand

Washing of the hand is treated last because it is the first and the last act to perform at meal time. It is compulsory that before one begins to eat a morsel one must first wash only the right hand which is used for eating. The same act must be performed after the meal. This food hygiene knows no age as both adults and children must wash their hands before and after a meal. The reason for this borders on hygiene. The right hand used for eating must have been variously soiled before meal time and as such has to be washed before eating. After meal the same thing happens since the hand has been smeared with food.

The left hand is not washed along with the right. If anybody does so he would be asked to throw away the water and replace it for others to use. The reason is that after using the toilet, one uses the left hand to handle leaves or toilet paper to clean the anus. Even where water is used it is the left hand that will touch the anus. So, to wash both hands for a meal is to 'pollute' the water to the annoyance of other participants at the meal.

This is because only one container is used to hold the water for those who are going to eat. That is the practice. In most cases the same water that is used at the beginning of the meal is used at the end of the meal. However, sometimes it is changed, depending on how dirty it is.

Invitation to a Meal

While a Yoruba family or person is having a meal and a visitor enters it is customary that either the father, the mother or the most senior of those who are eating invites the visitor by saying, *E wáa jeun* (come and eat). The visitor here does not necessarily mean a stranger; he could be a close relation, a friend or a neighbour coming in at the time of the meal. On rare occasions would the visitor actually accept to eat with them. The usual response is for the visitor to decline and thank the eaters to indicate that he would not participate. If the visitor is a youth he will say *A dúpé. Mo ti jeun* or *mo tí yó.* (Thank you; I have eaten or I'm fed). If he is an adult or an elderly person, and the eaters are a family with children he will say *Yóò gba ibi rere* or *Aràn rere ó gbà á* (Thank you. The food will land in safety). But if the eaters are a childless couple or if the woman is pregnant, the visitor will say *Omo o bá yín jé é* (Thank you. Your child will eat with you).

Should the visitor eat on invitation he would normally thank them after the meal but if he is elderly or just an adult he would add a prayer of blessing for his benefactors.

If the visitor is billed to stay with them till after the meal, the host (at meal) would quickly arrange for some light refreshment for his guest. The Yoruba person considers it morally wrong for the host to carry on eating while a visitor looks on! The host would not be comfortable to continue eating. At worst, he would suspend eating to attend to his visitor even though he may just have started eating.

Chapter 5

Playing Host

The Yoruba culture overtly supports playing host to other people. It seems that the people are more sociable than most other people of the world and this is why in all their formations (villages, towns, cities, etc) there are uncountable numbers of places where social parties are held at least weekly all the year round.

There are two types of host playing. The first is when one opens his door to other people for a party he sponsors. The party could be either in one's residence or at a neutral venue like a hotel and or public place. In the second type, one allows a visitor or stranger to dwell temporarily with one either for a few hours, a couple of days or a longer period of time.

Host playing are in two aspects. The first is the host and the other the guest. The host could be an individual (usually) or a group of people like a cultural society, religious group or even a political body. The guest could similarly be an individual or a group of people as stated above. In that case, such people must be known friends and relations.

The purposes of the foregoing is to enable us outline the cultural responsibilities of the host and the guest at a stretch.

The Host

To host a meeting, be it social or cultural, is to hold a party because after the meeting people could be hungry and it is a cultural necessity for the Yoruba to feed his guest, regardless of whether the guest is hungry or not. So, apart from preparing a venue for the meeting, arrangements must be made for feeding, at least, for light refreshments. It is also a common practice that if you must feed a group or an individual there must be enough to eat. This is the reason why people often borrow money and food to feed their guests. Some go into 'èsúsú' contribution and use its proceeds to host guests at a fixed party. The Yoruba are very hospitable. If any of the guests have a personal obligation to perform in the area and this comes to the knowledge of his host, the latter will willingly render assistance in whatever form he can - no matter the cost in time and material. The custom is that a guest must be comfortable at all costs. While pleasing his guest the host must do so willingly, cheerfully and without any reservation.

The second type of guest is the unexpected one who could either be a known person or a complete stranger. The guest would be warmly welcomed and well catered for throughout his stay - no matter the duration of the visit. The guest must be comfortable with his host. When departing he sees him off cheerfully.

There is an act of sincere generosity which to the non-Yoruba may look flattery. It is that the host will protest at the departure of his guest, begging him to stay a little longer. Even if the guest is a 'passer-by' the host would insist that he should stay. If the guest is in a hurry his host would entreat him to wait a while to dine with him even though he (the host) may be badly broke (in cash and material things) yet, he will beg him to wait. If the guest yields to his host's pressure and finally decides to wait, his host will run helter-skelter to find a way of satisfying him. He could even borrow either food items or the money to buy it. It is the practice of the Yoruba that they easily and readily lend money or material items to someone wishing to entertain a visitor or a stranger.

The general belief could be on religious grounds. It is said that if you take care of strangers you are working towards a caring treatment for yourself whenever you become a stranger somewhere. This practice is similar to that of the old Jews as it is written in the Bible where it is credited to God that man must adequately care for strangers.

Parting Gift

Another act of generosity by the host is that where it is necessary he would ensure that his guest departs with a gift after all the lavish treatment accorded him. The gift varies as to the environment. A farmer would insist his guest departs with farm products while an urban dweller would choose any form of city presents. He may also pay the transport fare of his guest if he does not refuse him.

The Guest

He could be a stranger or a known visitor who is either expected or unexpected. Guests at social parties, as treated in a previous chapter must show courtesy. A small percentage of the guests at social parties would give a token money indirectly to the host. Thus, if it is a childnaming ceremony they would give the mother some token money to receive on behalf of the child who is the *de jure* host. If it is a marriage ceremony such a token goes to the bride but if it is a burial occasion for a father or mother, the gift goes to the children of the deceased. That is, the particular child (of whatever age) of the deceased who invited the guests. So it is for each of the children according to the number and calibre of his guests at the ceremony. While the host does not invite his guests to dine and wine for a fee, yet, they should by tradition, show appreciation that he has spent a lot to host them.

Having discussed group guests, let us examine individual guests. They are of three types - familiar, known and the complete stranger.

The familiar guest is one that is well known to his host. He could be a friend or a close relation. Such a guest needs no protocol. In fact, he himself knows he would not be accorded any special reception. The familiar guest behaves as if he lives with his host.

The known guest could be a friend from abroad or just an acquaintance from another village, town or city. Then comes the stranger whom one has never met but who finds himself in a situation where he has to stay with his emergency host either for a few hours or a couple of days. The last two types of guests must reciprocate the fine treatment accorded them. Reciprocal gesture in this regard has nothing to do with money. It has to do with attitude and behaviour. He will greet every member of the host's family with great respect. He will thank his host so much and say nice things about the family. It is just part of guest-host nicety.

The guest will ensure that he does not exhibit any negative attitude like being angry nor pass negative comments, especially on the host's children who may at times appear inadvertently naughty. If the need arises he would rather pacify feuding kids than turn himself into an outright judge. Where necessary he would make corrections, with courtesy, to avoid negative actions or comments that may likely bring him in to collision with the children and their parents.

Chapter 6

Group Acts

The Yoruba are a highly gregarious race. Let us start from the family level. Whenever a father or mother is going on a social outing, like visiting a relation or a friend or even going to join other friends at an appointed place, he or she will not go out alone. If there is no friend nearby to go with, he or she will go with either one of their children or 'borrow' a child of that age from a neighbour for companionship. A Yoruba person does not want to go about alone but in the company of friends or relatives. This does not necessarily mean that he would bear the cost (he may or may not) yet the accompanying friend will not complain of the cost once they have agreed to go. Till today this tradition still exists. A youth would like to move about among his many friends. This practice is magnified by wealthy people and traditional leaders in the society who do social outings amidst retinues of friends and subordinates.

Apart from social outings promoting personal aggrandisement the Yoruba have formal groups catering for different facets of life. Five of these will be treated here - three are for the group labour and two are either economic or social. For group labour there are *àáaró, ọwẹ̀* and communal labour. The economic one is *èsúsú* and the social group is called *ẹgbẹ́*.

Àaró

It is simply a reciprocal labour arrangement among friendly neighbours. It is practised mainly among farmers whereby two or more persons work an equal number of days in rotation on each member's farm. The members are small in number so that the arrangement may not cause each to be absent from his own farm for too long. In such a mutual practice, there are no renegrades unless as a result of an accident or death. What brings them together is work and so each of the members of the *àaró* group really works hard to justify the reason for their decision to work together. In the majority of instances, *àaró* groups do not make plans for sumptuous formal meals outside refreshments during afternoon break which is usually very short. They work till sunset when they disperse to their individual homes for supper.

Ọwẹ

Ọwẹ is another manual work arrangement. The difference between it and àaró lies in the large size of Ọwẹ group and that it is not necessarily reciprocal. Ọwẹ is an arrangement whereby a man who has a very difficult task to perform enlists the assistance of the whole community - usually a whole village and friends in neighbouring villages. Thus, able bodied workmen assemble at a given date for the work. Nobody ever refuses participation. People have even expressed friendly anger if they were not invited. They cancel previous personal appointments to take part in Ọwẹ. Only on rare cases would those invited fail to partake, as they may in future need similar assistance.

Another interesting feature of Ọwẹ is that those who were invited but who would not be available on the fixed day would come penultimately or later to do their portion of the task.

Ọwẹ can be used to execute a number of personal tasks. These are mainly agricultural - clearing of farmland, making heaps or ridges, weeding or harvesting. It is also used to build (mould) houses. Before the advent of cement blocks the Yoruba made use of beaten earth to mould walls for their houses.

Communal Work

Aáró and Ọwẹ are personalised as individuals organise them with selected members of the community. Communal tasks are organised to provide social amenities for a particular community or village. The Báálê or other accredited leaders in the area harangue the people for compulsory manual work on given dates to provide particular facilities such as digging a drawing point on a local river or brook where women can fetch water for domestic use. It is also used to dig canals for a marshy community, and the like. However, well digging does not fall within communal work because only specialists can do it. Before the advent of motorable roads, it used to be footpaths leading from one village to the other. The footpath system still exists in villages till date, especially to link either farms, barns or smaller villages where there are no motorable roads. Thus, the network of footpaths across the nation or in each of the smaller communities are results of communal work. There is a third object of communal work. It is the erection of public buildings whether for recreation or for residences for friendly strangers visiting the community.

These were usually found in villages and not in the cities. Some villages housed their teachers in communally built guest houses.

Advance Work

Where it is impossible for one or two people to be present to work with others on the task day they are allowed to carry out their portion of the task in advance. Thus, before embarking on such task they must seek the indulgence of the village head. They could perform their own self-assigned portion of the work one or two days to the fixed date.

Treating Cheats

It is true that people do not easily cheat in communal work performance. This is probably because the task concerns everybody. For example, if it is cutting or clearing of a water way or making a water drawing point, everybody needs water for domestic use. If it is road work everybody walks on the road. Who then would say the task concerned does not effect him? Yet, there are cheats. They become cheats because they cannot reasonably defend their absence at the task. What the community does is to sanction them or call them for public reproach. In the case of public reproach the cheats are called out and carpeted; rebuked to the point of ignominy. The parents of such youths go about in shame; almost as outcasts - though they regain their socialisation status after a few weeks.

If the punishment is a fine, what is done is that the people will seize any domestic animal in the name of the cheat and consequently direct the owner of the animal to the cheat or his family for payment. The cost of animals seized is usually commensurate with the fine the cheat is expected to pay. In extreme cases such animals are slaughtered and the meat is shared. But in most cases the seizure is meant to embarrass the cheat thereby making his parents plead for their racalcitrant child. It is also a form of disgrace that is capable of making the family social lepers, at least, for a period.

It is this social implication that makes people register their presence at all costs whenever there is a communal job to be done.

Presence of Elders

It is William Shakespeare who said, 'They also serve who only stand and wait'. He used this witty expression as if he knew what occurred and still continues in a Yoruba cultural set up. During the execution of communal work elderly people in the community are found moving around, encouraging

the workers. They greet them and where necessary cast jokes to enliven the atmosphere, thus making people work harder in a relaxed mood. Some old men may see a twig blocking the way and remove it. If they see a stone capable of causing harm on the road, they remove it. An elderly man would caution a particular worker to be careful at a particular point he considers dangerous. So, old men go about to make their presence felt. They may advise as to the extent of the task and the time work should stop. They may encourage younger ones or women to fetch water for the workers to quench their thirst. Thus, everybody in the community is involved in the communal task, one way or the other. Those elderly ones who are unable to be physically present because of ill health or old age would send messages of apology to their colleagues on the site and such messages are normally accepted .

Similarly, the elders are also present at *ọwẹ* sessions because of the magnitude of workmen involved.

Back-up Drumming
The talking-drum is a great heritage of the Yoruba. The drummer sounds his drum to transmit a message or to praise individuals or families. So, during communal tasks that involve a particular village or community the drummers, like the elders, are also present as a mark of solidarity with those performing the task. The act is equally encouraging to the workers. The persons who often drum for them at leisure occasions and social gatherings are also around to enliven the atmosphere. As their profession dictates, all drummers know the personal eulogies of every family in the community. So he drums to praise family heads or members who are present at the work site. As the communal task progresses the drummer beats free of charge for the participating wokers in appreciation of their efforts.

The drummer takes the participants one by one for the praise-drumming. The effect is that people work harder and longer with the talking drum magic. In fact, the talking drum boosts the ego of the one being praised and gives him a larger than life impression of himself.

Èsúsú or *Àjọ*
Èsúsú is a thrift arrangement of periodic financial contributions agreed upon by a group of participators. They are limitless in number - ranging from two to one thousand or more. Under it a group of friendly individuals may decide to contribute the same amount of money either daily, every market day (that is, every fourth day), weekly or monthly. After the collection one of them will

take the contributions or sometimes it is shared between two members. This will go round every contributor but at different occasions. It is a co-operative society and not a banking business because the contributions are taken each time by one or two members with nothing left in the purse for any other purpose. Also, the contribution does not yield interest. It is a system created to assist members solve their financial problems.

Before the arrival of the white man who brought christianity and the seven-day week system, the most popular period measurement was the market day. So *èsúsú* meetings and the contributions used to take place mainly on market days, that is, every fourth day.

By culture, the Yoruba are faithful to whatever course they are pursuing or that has been commonly agreed upon. Thus, blacklegs are not common, yet they manifest on few instances. The success of any *èsúsú* organisation hangs on how faithful and trustworthy the members are. This is because members who benefit from the *èsúsú* proceeds early face great temptation of possible default for the simple reason that immediately one takes the contribution and spends it the system becomes a debt on that member. There have been cases where people paid such debt for a period of three years, that is, the period the particular *èsúsú* arrangement lasted. So, if early beneficiaries do not fraudulently withdraw it means every member will enjoy the system fully. It was rare to have defaulting members in the good old days . That time if a man died after having benefited from the *èsúsú* proceeds his children would take up the payment until the last member would have taken his turn.

Sadly, there are reported cases in modern times when some members absconded to unknown places to avoid paying back. Many a member has travelled overseas unannounced after having gathered his own *èsúsú* proceeds. In modern times a number of *èsúsú* organisations have collapsed because of the unfaithfulness and fraudulence of some of their members. Such cases are however very few. Unfortunately, it is uncommon to have such people taken to court. This may probably be so because nobody wants to invest in court proceedings which are often costly and long drawn. Some of those indicted have resorted to *jùjú* (African occult) to obtain retribution.

Because of the fear of being defrauded the number of elitist groups involved in *èsúsú* is limited to colleagues who draw their salaries from the same employer. If any outsider has to be included then an insider-guarantor will have to sponsor his membership. Friendly members of the same profession still constitute themselves into an *èsúsú* organisation.

Proceeds

In the olden days the *èsúsú* organisation was not always targetted towards events in which members needed money. Today, some members take permission to fix their turn of collection at a time of need. In past years some *èsúsú* contributions lasted two to five years. In modern times, things are different. Nobody wants to take part in any *èsúsú* arrangement that is likely to last beyond one calender year. There are six months special target *èsúsú* arrangements. Where every member or the majority are salary earners they are likely to terminate it between nine to ten months, probably, to end before December so as to have some breathing space. When the circle is short the yoke of long drawn debt repayment will be avoided.

Many *èsúsú* arrangements come into being these days because one or two people are planning ceremonies in which they hope to spend a lot of money. What they do is to campaign to convince others to join in the system. Such ceremonies include marriage, burial, property acquisition and child naming. They convince the number of people that they believe can honestly take part while they make their interest known as to when they would like to take their own turn of the contribution.

Some of those who do not have any special project in mind take part in *èsúsú* because it is an opportunity for them to save, especially salary earners and traders. Many families take part in *èsúsú* for domestic reasons. Perhaps, not for daily feeding but for annual purchase of clothes for their children and to buy some other items to mark certain anniversaries like Easter, Christmas, Id-ed-fitri or Id-el-kabir, etc.

Bàbá Alájọ System

We have discussed *èsúsú* by communal practice or by consensus. There is also the *Bàbá alájọ* system. This one exists among marketmen and women or petty traders generally. Under this system there is a man who turns himself into a professional *èsúsú* collector. His collection frequency ranges from daily, every other day, every market day to weekly contributions. He goes round his customers, that is, his own *èsúsú* members, with his big note book full of names arranged like a school register of attendance. The *Bàbá Alájọ* or *èsúsú* collector, has different books for members taking part in different collection frequencies. Thus, there is a book for daily contributors and different ones for other periods.

In this case there is no limit to the number of members since the collection is being handled by a professional man and not just somebody acting for his group of friends on an *ad hoc* basis. The number of members depend on how far the professional collector can reach to solicit for membership and his capacity to service them adequately, relative to the frequency. Each of his clients has a card which he marks to conform with the general register in his possession. If it is a daily one the client may pay for a certain number of days in advance, anticipating or taking care of days of sales recession or when he may not be available.

Collecting the proceeds varies from client to client. If for example it is a daily *èsúsú* arrangement, a client may decide to collect her òwn proceeds at the end of each week to take care of certain weekend expenses. He may decide to make it monthly or even fortnightly. The basic fact in this type of *èsúsú* system is that participants fall into the group of petty traders who do not patronise any bank probably because of daily low market proceeds or because the majority of them are illiterate.

The *Bàbá alájó* system is different from the former one. While the communal one carries neither interest nor commission the professional collector (*Bàbá alájó*) system carries a commission. Thus, if it is a daily contributor and a client saves say ₦2 every day the collector may settle for ₦2 per week. In that case, to complete a week a client will have to pay an extra day so that eight days make her own week. Those on weekly *'èsúsú'* have their own commission terms and those of other frequencies have also theirs.

Personality of *Bàbá Alájó*

Before canvassing for *èsúsú* clients, the modern day collector will display his company's registration certificate and his contact address.

However, it is not common to have a *Bàbá alájó* abscond with his clients' money. Though it has happened, but in rare cases. Thus, it takes faith and courage on the part of the contributor to agree for someone to be 'hiding' her money in the name of collection. But the traditional Yoruba woman is ever trusting. She does not doubt the integrity of the man. Thus, it is the absolute trust which clients always have in the *Bàbá Alájó* that writes the success of the system. It is the commission from his client that the *èsúsú* collector has lived upon from time immemorial. The additional gain that could accrue to him in the modern times is that he can earn interest if he deposits his clients' money into his personal bank account.

The only thing gained by the client is that her money is safe and can be retrieved any time it is needed. That is why she rather pays for the service rendered to her by way of commission to the *Bàbá Alájó*.

Today, the *èsúsú* system cuts across diverse ethnic backgrounds. It has almost become a nationally accepted saving system.

Certain banks in Nigeria have designed a way of using the *èsúsú* system to make traders save money with them. A good example is the community banks which are actually meant for the categories of people who patronise *èsúsú* arrangements.

Ẹgbẹ́

Like others discussed earlier, the name *Ẹgbẹ́* is retained in its vernacular form so as to preserve its meaning from being eroded or corrupted in the process of direct translation into English. *Ẹgbẹ́* could broadly be interpreted to mean society, group, communal association or group of friends united for a common course. Apart from the seemingly unending meanings, *Ẹgbẹ́* also has many features or forms. A thrift group comes under it and so also do small or large numbers of people who meet periodically, a small group of friends who decide to buy and wear the same type and colour of clothes, an *èsúsú* group, groups of youths of the same age range, a secret society, people of the same profession and so on. In other words, *Ẹgbẹ́* is synonymous with bodies like society, group, association, organisation, union and company in every way they can be used.

Besides the gregarious implications of its meaning and what it stands for *Ẹgbẹ́* is primarily a social organisation. This *Ẹgbẹ́* being discussed is set up by friends merely for social interaction. It is often very unwieldy to the extent that the members may not know each other as they ordinarily should. They meet periodically on market days, weekly, monthly, fortnightly, quarterly or annually. There is a fixed amount payable by every member at every meeting. In the traditional set up the officers are almost permanent. They normally conduct elections but the social standing of the Chairman always qualifies him for the post. The officers are not usually many. After the Chairman they could elect the secretary, the treasurer and the social secretary who is always described as the group's messenger (*sárẹ́-pẹgbẹ́*). They are likely to remain as officers till they can no longer cope with the task or are no longer available to render service. Incidentally, as every member gives due respect and regard to them, the officers themselves are not known to abuse their offices by being high-handed nor would they impose themselves on members, nor engage in financial mismanagement. However, modernity brings abuse of office and constant elections.

Fine imposition often causes chaos and rowdiness in certain *Egbé* meetings while it is treated jokingly in others. For example, absence from meetings attracts a fine. Some defaulters plead for forgiveness and are forgiven after giving good reasons for their action, some pay outright while others either pay grudginly or start arguments which often waste meeting times. This is why many societies are wary of imposing fines.

The questions then arise: what are the responsibilities of members to their *Egbé?* And what does one gain from membership? A member is expected to attend all the meetings punctually but where attendance is impossible the leadership would have to be informed in advance. Where sitting levies are charged it is compulsory for every member to pay. Loyalty to the course of the organisation is necessary as it is with any other human groups. Every member is expected to be the spokesman for the organisation whenever the image of the body is under scrutiny. If any communal task is at stake every member must be involved in its execution. Where personal involvment is impossible the member concerned either takes excuse in advance or sends word to the leadership during task operation or buys his way by sending some refreshments which is accepted on merit and not just as it is presented. This is to discourage others from dodging responsibilities via such an avenue in future.

If a member is playing host for a marriage, burial or dead person's remembrance, etc. he will be expected to invite other members via the Chairman. Members are obliged to do two or all of three things. They could collect special levies (if such has not been included in their sitting levies) to prepare food and buy drinks to serve themselves at that venue. They may collect another money to give to their host during the course of the ceremony.

Therefore, the main gain of a member from the *Egbé* is the solidarity with him whenever he is performing social ceremonies. Thus, he has some people ready to rejoice or console with him at appropriate times.

Egbéjodá

This is often mistaken for *Aso Ebí* in many areas, particularly within the elitist society. It is a sort of uniform worn by members of a particular society. Whenever a member of the society has a ceremony he would want as many people as possible to identify with him and so he chooses a particular colour and pattern of cloth which all his friends would wear at the occasion. It is this uniform that is called *egbéjodá*. The one worn exclusively by many members of the same family is known as *aso ebí*.

46

In some traditional Yoruba societies this society uniform is given another name apart from *Ẹgbẹ́jọdá*. It is called *Aṅkóò* which is coined from the English expression 'And Co', with 'Co' standing for company. When they express it they say *kó aṅkóò* meaning 'taking part in wearing particular clothes as a society or group uniform'. And when they refer to the cloth itself they call it the cloth of *aṅkóò* (*aso aṅkóò*).

The reasons for organising *egbẹ́jọdá* or *aṅkóò* have been mentioned, that is, to celebrate a ceremony or mark an event in a colourful or grand fashion. Another reason is fellowship. By that, a group just decides that during an annual celebration members should all wear the same type of clothes without anybody being the centre person or the host. In that case they may decide that every member must put on the same clothes for the first time on the day of the occasion like Easter, Christmas, Eid-el-kabir or *Egúngún* (in Ọ̀yọ́ area) *ọlọ́jọ́* (in Ilé-ifẹ̀) or *Ẹ̀yọ̀* (in Lagos).

Participation by individual members in *aṅkóò* is implicitly compulsory. Nobody ever compels others to participate but the thought is that 'if I do not participate in Mr *Lágbájá's aṅkóò* when my turn comes he may not take part'. This explains why you have so many people getting involved.

There are degrees of participation in *aṅkóò*. There is full dress participation and there is the cap participation. By full dress is meant clothing from top to toe as mentioned earlier. The cap participation is sparingly done in rural areas but in metropolitan communities like Lagos, Ìbàdàn, Abẹ́òkúta, etc. the two go hand in hand. 'Capping' means cap only for men and *gèlé* (head gear) only for ladies. So ceremonies become colourful with nearly everybody putting on the same kind of attire.

The Celebrant

There are only two points to discuss concerning the celebrant. The first is in dressing and the second is in the celebrant's dance.

The type and the number of clothes for use during a particular ceremony depends on whether or not the celebrant is a man or woman. If he is a man he will not dress lavishly. If there is a common cloth selection for the ceremony he wears it. If there is no cloth selection for the occasion he wears one of his best clothes. The celebrant does not necessarily have to change his dress. Thus, the male celebrant is not particular about his dresses. In most cases the wife pressurises him to use particular clothes or to change dresses at intervals during the ceremony. Generally, men do not 'worship' clothes.

47

Where the celebrant is a woman one must expect colour - clothes display or 'art festival'. Within the few hours of the party she can change her dresses as often as she pleases. In the same way she changes her handbags, and her jewllery and shoes. The Yoruba woman could be colourful when she is throwing a social party!

The celebrant's dance is an important item in the programme of a social party. The sole objective is to rake in some money from guests, especially friends, associates and relations who are present. The amount of money to be collected depends on the celebrant's popularity, the quantity and quality of food served at the party. That means, a popular celebrant who serves a sumptuous meal and has invited many important personalities will thus reap a lot of money to defray part of the cost of the party. This practice today is an abuse of what it used to be.

Cloth Selection
Cloth selection is basic to *egbéjodá* or *ankóò*. As soon as the celebrant decides to mark his ceremony with *ankóò* he then selects the type of cloth he considers could be obtained in large quantities. Sometimes when the quantity is exhausted from the source of purchase an alternative is selected thereby making two types of cloth in circulation for the same ceremony. This is multiplicity by accident. There is multiplicity by design. There are two ceremonies that are capable of coming under such planned cloth multiplicity. The first is marriage. If the parents of the celebrant (the bride or the groom) have many grown-up children who are either all working or are wealthy, each child can select his own type of cloth for his friends to buy. The same thing happens if the ceremony is a burial or a remembrance of dead parents. Under the latter, the children who are celebrants may decide to select another type of cloth exclusively for themselves and their own children in addition to the multiple ones which relate to each of them. It is the common one or *asọ ẹbí* that they would wear during the celebrant's dance.

Ceremonies where cloth selection is necessary for planned *ankóò* are freedom from artisan apprenticeship, academic graduations, child-naming and house-warming (that is, when a new building is being declared open formally). Others are anniversaries (like christian, moslem and traditional festivals), welcoming special visitors to the community and political identification. The last three have no celebrants but organisers and the cloth is always one uniform.

The Party

Social parties last for only one day or less but preparations and rounding off can extend certain parties to three or more days. Where visitors from neighbouring towns or abroad must attend, such people would arrive before the party day and may not depart until one or two days latter. That means the celebrant must continue to feed and accommodate the visitors till their departure. This is why some celebrants continue to spend money for upward of one week, even though party attendants from the same community spend only a few hours.

In relation to party hours, there are types of party durations. There is the zero party occasion. By this, a family naming their new baby will embark only on a low-keyed ceremony whereby visitors come in, eat and go - usually the guests trickle in between noon and six o'clock in the evening.

The second is the day party for which visitors could arrive as from noon and could end between seven and eight o'clock in the night. The third type is the evening party which could last from five to nine or ten o'clock in the night. This last type is the all-night party. Attendants to such a party begin to arrive from eight in the night while the party lasts till four or five o'clock the following morning.

Except the zero party system the other three types have their individual peaks. The peak period is when the celebrant takes the party floor dance. Where there is more than one celebrant and each has his or her own circle or gathering within the same big party, each of them will dance in his or her own circle. Where there is only one celebrant for a large sprawling party he may decide to dance in one or two places as word is passed round so that people might go to honour him whenever he dances.

The peak time for a day party could be any time between three and four o'clock in the afternoon. For a night party it could be between eight and nine o'clock in the night while it could be two or three a.m. for an all-night party. It depends on the celebrants.

It is interesting to note that every party attendant expects the peak time when the celebrant must dance. In most cases, attendants urge the celebrant to do his dancing because they are eager to leave the party venue. On many occasions, immediately the celebrant finishes dancing many of the guests begin to depart.

Sàráà

A thanksgiving party otherwise called *Sàráà* in Yoruba is one which is held to feed people after one has survived either a serious illness, an accident or any disaster which could have killed or maimed one for life. What the guests at such parties usually do is to pray and rejoice with the host for surviving whatever ordeal he had gone through. It is an eat and go party. No dancing either.

Party Gifts

Most of the guests at a party usually give their hosts some money before departure. Such monetary gifts are in two categories. In the first category close friends or even relatives of the host may decide to assist him with fairly large sums of money so that he could defray part of the debts incurred in the process or for him to make the party grand. But anybody wishing to lend him money voluntarily would have done so days or weeks before the party or just before the party begins.

The second category of party gift falls within the token gift. Everybody that attends a social party is supposed to give some money no matter how little. Therefore the majority of those who give party gifts are token givers. Some of the people in this category give in accordance with the quality of food or volume of drinks they have consumed. It must be stated that the gifts are voluntary. As a matter of courtesy the host would say appropriate greetings to those guests who gave him gifts. He may say: 'Thanks for spending' or just, 'Thank you for the gift'. If he is the one that lent him a huge amount of money he may say, *E kú ináwó* (Thanks for the sum lent me).

Reciprocal Gifts

The reciprocal gift is the modern addition to party benefits. It is a sort of 'thank you gift' from the host to the guests or attendants. This practice was started in the early sixties by which the host presents gifts to their guests and other party attendants. It began with only those who bought and put on the *egbéjodá* otherwise called *ankóò*. But now everybody attending the party goes away with as many gifts as to the number of givers from the host's family and friends. The gifts could be plastic materials, stationery, handkerchiefs, cutlery, etc. Thus, only money is presented to the host by some but everybody receives a material gift for attendance beside eating and drinking!

Types of Parties

Again, the Yoruba throw the following types of social parties - marriage, child naming, burial and graduation from apprenticeship. The latter is popularly called 'freedom'. Added to these in the modern sense are birthday, death anniversaries and wake-keeping ceremonies. For example, wealthy and influential persons throw parties to mark their birthdays while many that have the means now celebrate promotions and appointments.

Chapter 7

Sympathy

The Bible says that we should weep with those who are weeping and rejoice with those who are rejoicing. By sheer coincidence the Yoruba do that normally. When a thing of joy happens they celebrate it abundantly and when sorrow creeps in they truly share it solemnly with the victim.

Situations demanding sympathy vary from minor to grave. The rate at which the Yoruba express kind words and pleasantries is the same as the rate they express sympathy or pity, depending on which of the two situations occurred at that particular moment. If somebody has a sharp mosquito bite-since it often results in sudden sharp pain which causes instant but jerky reaction by the victim - everybody around will sympathise with him. Everybody, young or old, friend or foe, would almost chorus the word of pity - *pèlé* or *e pèlé*, which simply means 'sorry', but which literally means 'gently', an expression towards caution. That sharp reaction by the victim of the mosquito bite automatically transmits an emotion of sympathy for pain round those present at the time. In expressing pity to the victim various sympathisers will give different suggestions as to what one could do either to avoid future bites or get rid of mosquitoes, even up to the history of mosquito bites. Some would prescribe how to cure the effect of the bite.

When a person knocks his foot against a hard object or steps upon a sharp instrument that cuts his foot, the expression of sympathy is relatively as great as the facial expression of pain. This produces a sight that inspires great pity in those present. As long as the victim either displays the feeling of pain or the onlooker sees the wound on the victim, the sympathising words of *pèlé or e pèlé* will continue to be heared. Immediately an accident occurs sympathisers swing into action - applying first aid; how to remove any foreign body that may be lodging in the body via the spot of injury. Even if those present are strangers they will still continue to render brotherly assistance till the victim is in direct contact with his family or friend who would take over from them. Thus, sympathy is neither casual nor superficial in the Yoruba man or woman. There are degrees of injuries that impel different degrees of emotion in the sympathisers; sorrow or even weeping, even where the victim himself can endure the pain. The mere sight of the injury of a certain degree drives some sympathisers to almost a state of coma. One can talk of coma in this sense where the display of sorrow by the sympathisers is watched by all. Not just that, the sympathiser may be so disturbed that he might not be able to do any other thing for some time. He may even lose appetite for a greater part of the day.

Certain categories of accidents bring about the degree of sympathy being described. They include accident like road mishap, falling from a tree, a tall building or a ladder, being a victim of an accidental discharge, deep matchet or axe cut and dangerous burns. Since the Yoruba are highly sociable the house or the clinic where the victim is being treated would automatically become a pilgrimage point with relations, colleagues, friends and foes alike going to say 'sorry get well'. If the victim could not be reached because of the degree of the injury, sympathisers will ensure they see either a relation or friend of the victim to express their sympathy through that person, or people, as the case may be. In fact, the family of the victim will station people at a strategic place to welcome sympathisers on behalf of their injured kin. Such people would take note of the callers and report their visit to the injured man whenever he recuperates.

As the sympathisers flock to the victim's house many of them would come with one material gift or the other. These could be cash, medication and other relevant materials. Some will even send native medicine, whether material or incantational, direct to the victim to assist him recover quickly. Some will pray for the victim either privately or openly among their church congregations or moslem jamas.

Fire Disaster

Let us examine the way people sympathise with somebody whose house has been razed by fire.

A victim of a fire disaster could spontaneously respond to the misfortune in any of three ways: He could be the type who is so perplexed and out of his senses that he can only manage to salvage an old cloth or any insignificant material. It has happened that such category of victim goes out with just a plate or pot as a display of his emotional confusion. Secondly, the victim could be the fatalistic type who resigns himself to fate. The third type could be the one ready to die in the inferno because of his stupid courage to

53

salvage some valuables or for the love of certain family members trapped in the inferno. In most instances the later does not live to be consoled.

The three situations stated above determine the depth of sympathy to be expressed to a victim of a fire disaster. The fourth situation is that of one whose building is a bit far from the source of conflagration by a distance of a number of houses and so he has the time to salvage very important goods from his house before the flames get there.

Let us assume that the four types of persons whose pictures are painted above have their houses razed by fire. However, only the fourth person has his house burned down after he has evacuated most of his valuables. The other three lost everything. In addition one of them has lost a relation in the fire while the other has almost an empty house.

Consolation

When it comes to sympathising with or consoling, the three categories have some things in common. All of them attract sympathy from members of the public including immediate neighbours and passers-by, either during the fire or after the house has been charred. In the case of the one whose relation died in the fire some of the sympathisers will also weep openly to express the depth of their sympathy. Wherever the victims stay as alternative abodes they will be frequented by sympathisers. Some of the very close ones will even stay with the victim during day time for about three days. The purpose of this is to be as close as possible to the victim to forestall either a suicide or an on uncontrollable self-pity which often results in starvation and physical deterioration, a sickness that could eventually lead to the death of the victim. So, when people stay with him they counsel him to be light minded about his loss. In fact, this type of method is also used for people who are bereaved.

Encouragement

Since the purpose of staying closer to the victim (or even the bereaved) is to encourage him, a number of methods are often applied to make him forget his loss or at least to spiritually discountenance it as àmúwá Ọlọrun, that is, an 'act of God'.

(1) Close neighbours will provide him with food as well as feed the sympathisers who have come to sympathise with him. This may continue for upward of a week depending on the depth of the loss and their relationship with the victim. Women will do the same thing for the victim's wife. Some close relations will also stay with him for a couple of days. At first some will be there throughout the day, later they would go to

their work and return in the evening. The victim may not make use of the food stuff donated to him by sympathisers until they cease to visit him.

(2) Money will also be given to him from various sources. If he has not got the proceeds of his *èsúsú* he may request for them and any verbal application would be considered because of his condition. Colleagues at his place of work will send him money if it is not possible for them to pay him a visit because of distance. Loan opportunities either by co-thrift or salary advance or both could also be opened to him so that he can rehabilitate fast.

(3) Those who come either to stay temporarily or to visit him briefly will tell him stories so that he may learn from the experiences of other people. Some of these will even strengthen him to regard his situation as milder and more tolerable. Some will tell stories that are so funny that everybody will reel with laughter, including the victim. The aim is to lift his spirit.

(4) Playing of games is another way of consoling the victim. Traditionally, *Ayò* used to be the only game played during such occasions but at a time there was a game called *gúdà* (dr) played in certain communities like Èrúwà in Ibarapa. This game was similar to draughts. Only in recent times do we have games like draughts, ludo, cards, etc. At first people will play the game near the victim so that he could see them in action and as the game progresses he would instinctively suggest steps to beat an opponent or to prevent a win. At last he also plays!

(5) There are extreme cases where the victim rejects all methods of spiritual or psychological rehabilitation and remains in mournful mood all the time. In such a case sympathisers tell the victim stories of extreme cases where the character either died or got maimed or suffered some sort of incapacitation because he refused people's entreaties. Then he is left to do whatever he likes himself. This will lead to him consoling himself shamefully and eventually going round to beg those whom he had disappointed. It will be noted that the five steps given above are often used to console bereaved people because situations of death are more common than that of fire.

Bereavement

Having said the above about bereavement one would just add an aspect of communal solidarity which forms part of sympathy. Thus, as people want to show that the loss suffered by the bereaved is also painful to them you see them wailing bitterly while some of the elders chant the praise names of the dead and eulogise his family which in turn makes the bereaved weep with the sympathisers! Thus, the whole area is filled with sobbing and wailing at intermittent times as different sympathisers come around wailing.

Deceptive Weeping

There is an interesting aspect of the wailing spree by certain sympathisers. Usually, people going to sympathise from the same compound or house do so in a group. It sometimes happens that a group will determine where or at what distance to the bereaved person's house they should begin to weep. So, when they get nearer the house all of them, will begin to wail 'bitterly'. People have heard them say 'let us begin from here', as if they have been compelled to weep. Another amusing antic of this group of sympathisers is that some of them often soak either their cap (for men) or head gear (for women) in water. As they 'cry bitterly' to rouse further feelings of sorrow from the relations of the deceased, they use the soaked cap to wipe off the tears. This happens usually when a very old person dies at 'a ripe age'. This deceptive practice is not easy to detect.

Burial Funding

By Yoruba practice, the death of an elderly relation that deserves a ceremonial burial always attracts easy loans. Out of sympathy for the bereaved most of such loans are unsolicited before being granted.

Chapter 8

Characteristics

The traditional Yoruba man or woman has a bundle of character traits that any good religion could pass for godliness. Some of these have been treated one way or the other in this book. Those treated include sympathy, gregariousness and hospitality.

(a) **Truthfulness** is a quality the traditional Yoruba man' does not compromise on. He does not care about the consequences of telling the truth, in fact, he is addicted to it. There is a saying that *Bí a bá so òtítọ́ a ọ́ kú, bí a kò so òtítọ́ a ó kù, kí á kúkú so òtítọ kí àdàbà ó fò* (if we tell the truth we will die, if we don't, we will die; why can't we then say the truth and let the dove fly). Dove flying means daring the consequence. Dying in the saying refers to an impossibility of eternity on earth for man. In other words, the saying warns one against telling lies, whatever the incentive. Every family trains the children to always tell the truth while children who tell lies are seriously scolded.

A general display of truthfulness among the generality of the Yoruba is seen in the idea of unmanned sale of certain essential goods. It was the practice before and a few years after independence in Nigeria, that farmers placed yams, bananas, garden eggs, pepper and other farm products by a busy roadside without anybody being physically present to sell the items. Instead, the amount at which the items were to be sold was placed there so that people wishing to buy could do so by the price tag. The owner would come later to collect the money without any kobo missing from the total amount! This practice is no longer in vogue in urban areas but only in parts of the countryside.

Despite the general inclination to truthfulness, there are people known for telling lies. What happens is that everybody knows such liars in the community and they are held with scorn. They are notorious among the people and live as bad examples.

57

(b) **Fairness and Objectivity** are similar qualities that form part of character traits of the traditional Yoruba. The traditional Yoruba man does not cheat whoever has anything to share with him. He prefers to cheat himself if what is available cannot be shared fairly, especially when the other party is not present. It is the same thing when it comes to his passing judgement on given issues, he sticks to objectivity and fairness. He would not want to be influenced to give a wrong judgement. He would not give his opinion until both sides of the issue in contention are made known, no matter the pressure. He prefers to withhold his views rather than be one-sided, probably because of some corrupt considerations. He believes that there is a superior being in the person of God who will rejudge bad judgements. A guiding proverb says, *A gbọ́ ẹjọ́ apákan dá àgbà òsìkà* (He who judges only from one-side evidence is the worst evil doer). Thus, he would not cheat his fellow man because his own child or relation is involved. This trait is very much alive today. It can be seen in two forms.

In the first place, if a Yoruba man heads an organisation he would want to display fairness by employing people of other ethnic nationalities, probably on equal basis so that he may not be accused of tribalism. It has happened that he appointed people from other tribes who later caused his sack or dismissal for flimsy reasons. The second example is the practice whereby Yoruba leaders are more criticised by Yoruba journalists and Yoruba owned media houses. This is also why media organisations that are controlled by Yoruba jurnalists are more critical of leaders they believe have not measured up to expectations in public office. It is unusual for them to pass wrong things for good no matter whose ox is gored. A few individuals however flout such norms today.

(c) Next to be considered is the trait of **hardwork and dedication to duty**. Customarily, the Yoruba person is hardworking and dutiful. They hate lazy persons and lay-abouts. The English proverb which says that 'what is worth doing at all is worth doing well' passes for the attitude of the Yoruba man to duty. His is, play when to play and work when to work. Anything half way to this is a lazy ideal. He trains his children to be hardworking and dutiful right from infancy.

(d) **Live and Let Live**: This is another traditional motto of the Yoruba person. He does not want to monopolise things or issues. He does not want his own right to jeopardise the right or comfort of others.

If what he enjoys would cause discomfort to others he would adjust immediately. There is a saying that spells this quality to the heart of the Yoruba person. It is commonly said that *Ẹnì kan kò dúró ní méjì-méjì* or *Igi kan kò di igbó* (No individual person can behave like a crowd). The saying means that consideration must also be given to other parties in the scheme of things at all times.

(e) **Kindness** is embedded in hospitality yet it stands out on its own. The Yoruba man or woman is kind and would promote kindness at every opportunity. There is a guiding proverb for kindness that says that *Bí o bá fẹ́ kí o sìkà, bí o bá rántí íkú Gáà kí ó sàánú* (if you so wish you could be cruel but if you remember the death of Gaa you should be kind). Gaa was the leader of the kingmakers in the old Oyo kingdom. He was said to be very cruel but was later slain and his flesh chopped into pieces to match his cruelty while alive.

(f) **The Yoruba is seniority conscious**. He does not want a junior person to perform what a senior person should do nor should a senior person usurp the role of a junior person. It borders actually on a sort of protocol. The idea is not inimical to the youth. For example, as it has been mentioned in a preceding chapter, at meal time a child is not supposed to take meat from the plate before his elders. Similarly, menial house chores meant for the young would never be alloted to an elderly person. This is adherence to the principle of proportional right.

(g) **The issue of retribution** otherwise known as the law of cause and effect is a guiding principle for the Yoruba. This principle influences his judgement, thinking, action and relationship with others. There is a saying that *Bí a bá ṣoore fún ènìyàn pupa ẹni dúdú á sàn an* (if you do good to a white man it is a black man that will repay you). This saying teaches that when you help somebody do not expect a reward from him. It is believed that an act of kindness done to someone in Zaria could be repaid at *Èrúwà* or *Abà*, depending on where the doer is seeking help for himself at a later time. In like manner a Yoruba man would want to assist the children of his neighbours or even those whose parents are not known to him so that his own children may also be assisted in a foreign land or distant community. This is the principle that makes all children the children of all parents. Thus, you do not have to discriminate in solving problems that may affect any child. This natural law does not permit a Yoruba man to cheat or maltreat a fellow man.

(h) **Acts of Insolence**: Insolence can only be committed by a younger person against an elder or a servant to his master but a curse from a child to a parent. The main reason is to make the youth respect his elders or a junior his senior and for a servant to demonstrate his obedience to his master. Thus, anything bordering on banality cannot occur between the two. The principle of insolence is that it segments out the responsibilities of the junior from those of the senior. It tames the youth to be subservient always to his elders. For example, he cannot perform a feat superior to that of an elderly person and openly lay claim to it without being accused of insolence.

All the misbehaviours that come under insubordination in official relations form part of the bundle of offences that culminate in insolence.

Let us examine some of the acts that pass for insolence:

(1) a youth calling an adult by name and a junior in an office calling a superior officer by name;
(2) a youth watching an elderly person carrying a load or perform an assignment which a junior should do;
(3) a junior using the banal 'you' for an adult *iwo* instead of *eyin;*
(4) a youth first stretching his hand out for a handshake with an elderly person;
(5) a junior to hand over anything to a senior with the left hand;
(6) a junior to scold or abuse a senior;
(7) a youth claiming equality with an adult;
(8) taking meat before an adult when at meal together;
(9) sitting where an adult should sit or wants to sit; and
(10) staring an adult directly in the face during a conversation or worse still when the junior one is being scolded by that adult, etc.

(i) *Alájọbí and Ilẹ̀ Ọrẹ̀:* these are very strong terms in the line of unimpeded retribution. *Alájọbí* is the god or spirit guarding or overseeing consanguinity or people of the same blood relationship, like brothers and sisters, parents and children, cousins, etc. It is applied when an unwritten agreement is being made. It borders on placing absolute confidence in each other. Thus, there is no swearing to any oath when the agreement is made. Literally *Alájọbí* is derived from *Àjọbí* meaning consanguinity or togetherness in blood or being of the same blood relationship. The Yoruba regard blood relations as a sacred phenomenon. Similarly Ilẹ̀-ọrẹ̀ passes for what has been said of blood relationship but is different

60

in the sense that it relates to a relationship between or among trusted friends - not acquaintances. The trust existing between friends equals the gravity of blood in families.

In the majority of cases, those who disappointed in agreements reached in either of the two situations get the wrath of nemesis. The effect could be instant or delayed - no jilt ever goes without retributive punishment. Some who go free have their offsprings punished in their place. This may sound unbelievable but it happens in real life.

(j) *Ẹlẹ́dà* (Creator or God): when God is seen as the universal spirit the Yoruba call him *Olọ́run* (Creator and owner of the universe or the heavens) but when he is related to individuals as their creator he is referred to as *Ẹlẹ́dà* (Creator). Because of this knowledge, an average Yoruba person would not deliberately cheat, do or say anything negative against a fellow being unless it is the truth. If the negative thing is grave but true he would not forget to, by way of swearing, say *'Mr Lágbájá* is not here but his *Ẹlẹ́dà* (creator) is here'. If someone tells a lie, for example, against a person who is absent, an eyewitness will remind the evil speaker that the *Ẹlẹ́dà* of that absent person is around. Because of *Ẹlẹ́dà* the strong would not deliberately cheat the weak and a master or boss would not maltreat his servant or subordinate.

(k) **Settlement of Issues**: the Yoruba people believe that there is no quarrel or disagreement that cannot be settled by negotiation. When a misunderstanding arises and either or both parties are heightening issues the people use a proverb *Ẹnu ni a ó fi sọ o, idí ni a ó fi jóko rẹ* the meaning of which is 'it is a matter to sit and talk over' Truly, disagreements of whatever magnitude can be settled by talking things over. The settlement could be as simple as the quarrel; it may also be as difficult as the depth of the squabble. Every quarrel is started through the action of a party, either by commission or by omission. Normally, the wronged person will demand a reason from the offender and it is the reply to such a query that determines whether things will escalate or simmer down. If issues result in physical fighting the Yoruba have four methods of quelling them:

(1) It takes an elderly person to shout at the fighters and have them separated immediately. In such a case the two parties must obey the elders' order.

(2) If they fail to separate as a result of a verbal order by an elderly person or friends then one or two people may physically separate them. This method is sometimes injurious to the peacemaker if the fight is violent.

(3) If the two fighters had begun with verbal aggression and abusive words and had also attracted a warning from an elderly person, yet the brawl still continues, the next thing is for an agile man to take a whip and wallop the two of them evenly till they are separated. This is corporal intimidation.

(4) The fourth method is the principle of 'let them fight it out'. The proverb matching such a principle translates to mean that one should not separate two fighters till they become tired. *(Bí kò bá rẹ ìjà a kìí là á)*. In the first type, one of the two fighters must have proved stubborn and refused to agree to a settlement while his opponent could be willing. If people see that the willing one could punish the stubborn one they will allow the fight to continue for a reasonable time and later separate them when the stubborn one must have been worn out. In the second type, if the two fighters are so hefty and masculine that peacemakers could get badly wounded separating them, they will allow the fight to drag on for a while. As they fight, it is not uncommon to see some women cry for their separation while some others weep as the fighting gets fiercer. At last, they get them separated and it is possible for either or both to get wounded or have their clothes badly torn.

Negotiation which the fighters refused to agree to at the beginning will still end it all. This is why there is a proverb which says that *Ọmọ àlè ni ó rí ìjá tí ó yẹ kí ó jà tí kò ní jà; ọmọ àlè ni à ńlà ní ìjà tí kìí gbọ́* (only a bastard sees the reason, to fight but fails to fight and he also is a bastard who disagrees to end fighting while being separated).

The Yoruba believe that only in extreme cases should a man fight since he, as a human being, can reason unlike the animal that has to fight and quarrel to obtain its right among colleagues.

(1) **Blind Collaboration:** A well bred Yoruba man would not take side in a fight of which he does not know the origin. If his blood relation or best friend is fighting someone else he would rather make an effort to separate and settle the matter for them than stupidly jump into the fray. The reasons for such a decision are that if his relation is guilty it would

be too bad for him to fight a wrong course and even if he is right, good reason does not permit him to lend support in a fight but to find a settlement. Finally, supposing the two of them die fighting, who will give account?

An average Yoruba person does not plan a fight against either a real or a perceived enemy for he believes that God in nemesis would catch up with anybody's enemy at any time. He would however avoid any contact with such an 'enemy' to avoid possible anger that may result in a fight. This is why some other people have wrongly dubbed the Yoruba man a coward. There is a proverb which says that a thoughtless valiant is worse than a weakling (*Alágbára má mèrò Bàbá òle*). The Yoruba person is highly critical of his brother who is not doing the right thing. Nature created them to be down to earth about truthfulness. He would not side his brother wrongly because he is his brother.

(m) **High Face Saving**: If a notable person like the Oba, a community leader, a socialite or some other respectable personality in the society mistakenly or even intentionally commits a wrong doing or an act which later results in a scandal, that person would simply take his own life to avoid the scourge of public disgrace. There is a saying that *Ikú yá ju èsín* (death is preferable to public ridicule). This principle informs his action. Incidentally, any body who learns about the death of that person would simply comment that he had done what a man should do in the prevailing circumstance.

If that person is an Oba he would perform the ritual of opening the royal calabash which spells death by suicide. Otherwise, it would be ridiculous for such a great personality to be jailed after the rigours of a court case. This is why the Yoruba always think carefully well before taking any action on certain matters. He calculates in reticence.

(n) **Family Name**: The family name is of great importance to the Yoruba people. If a youth proves naughty or otherwise in public or to an elderly person, the first two questions that would be asked of him are: Where is your family compound or house? Who is your father? This is why it is customary for Yoruba parents to give sound home education to their children. A general statement by parents to their children going into the world is, *Ránti omo eni tí iwo ise,* (Remember the son of whom you are). People take pride in marrying the son or daughter of certain families because of their good name – not wealth!

63

Somebody with good deeds is next to the king or Oba in recognition. People love him, not to share in his wealth if he is rich but for his goodness to the society. On the other hand, if a man is rich but his source of wealth is doubtful or is known to be dubious, the community would talk bad about him behind his back. They may not confront him but he would find himself being isolated from the people.

The essence of attaching importance to a family name is to ensure that every youth behaves rightly in and outside the family precints, either to confirm a good image or cancel a bad one.

(o) **Abuse**: Abuse is a negative culture common among the Yoruba. Within a family setting it is only seniors who can abuse juniors without any reprisal but not without indignation from the one who has been tongue-lashed. A junior who abuses his senior is subjected to reproach or corporal punishment. Youths of the same age brackets could abuse for fun or for a fight. Women also do the same. Only in extreme cases will a man abuse his wife and vice versa. Acts of abuse like the ones mentioned above are actually for corrective purposes.

Some people are natural abuse vendors right from their youth. The fact that they grow up still abusing people does not mean they were not reproached all along.

Sometimes groups of youths entertain themselves and others by abusing one another.

The subject of abuse on an individual could be an x-ray of the person's life style, hidden behaviour and traits as well as whatever physical deformity he may have. All negative circumstances surrounding the victim are also subject to abuse. These include his parents, his children, his failures in life and crimes committed, either open or hidden. Ordinarily, abuse is indecent and negative but can serve as a satirical and corrective purpose.

Eye Check

The Yoruba woman sometimes uses her eyes to communicate discipline to her children and wards. Training children with the eye check begins with the use of the whole face and voice. For example, when she disapproves of a particular manner or action of a child she uses her voice to express it and also adds a scowl so that the two methods emphasise her disapproval of the action or behaviour of the child. When she has a visitor and the child tries to be naughty or makes a silly demand, she quickly scowls, squints or turns her eyes in a peculiar way. She may even decide to size the child up from head to toe in a mood of melancholy. It usually works. Immediately the child obeys, the woman covers up quickly with a smile or a laugh, whichever is appropriate to the situation.

Some children may be stubborn and disobedient and would not be bothered by their parent's eye check. In such a situation either of three steps is taken, depending on the parent's disposition. She could accede to the child's stubborness calmly with pretentious friendliness at the moment. She could meet the child, gently lead him outside where she applies a friendly reproach to enforce her will, or she could talk harshly to the child in the presence of her guest to enforce the purpose of the eye check. However, only on rare occasions do children prove stubborn to eye checks.

Men also apply the eye check to enforce discipline. It is a method applied in public places to discipline one's children or wards when occasions demand it.

On the other hand, women exclusively use eye checks against their rivals or antagonists and even against men they consider inimical to their peaceful homes.

Chapter 9

Governance

An average Yoruba man knows he has some natural and societal authorities he must respect or serve. These are his father (or his mother), the *Baálẹ̀*, the *Ọba* (the king or whatever name a society gives its crown head or monarch). The other is the supreme being, God (or by whatever name given to God in different communities).

The Father
As treated in chapter one of this book under 'The family', the father's authority is not limited to his own offspring alone. He is the guardian of a number of wards living with him. Children from anywhere can domicile with him and be regards them as his children. Thus, the father serves as mentor to the categories of persons described above in the extented family system.

Baálé (Head of Compound)
The Baálé is the head of a house or compound. The traditional Yoruba architectural pattern of house grouping is the compound. A compound is a group of houses belonging to various families and was arranged (in those days) in a circular form. If the families are not too many their houses will be in a continuous circular form with each house having an opening leading into the inner open premises of the compound with one gate leading outside. Where there are many families the arrangement will still be circular but not continuous. There will always be a space within the compound. Primarily, the compound system enabled the people to have an intimate contact with each other so that whoever needed urgent help received it instantly. Thus, house burglary was not known in compound system . The families living together within the premises are not always blood relations. Often they come there from different places. Strangers living among them also flourish without any discrimination. In other words, most compounds are cosmopolitan; but as time goes on they all live like a family, doing things in common like that. There

are very many of such compounds in a town or city. Every compound is distinguished with a name, usually that of the oldest man among the first settlers of the house. And it shall remain so for ever. At any given time every compound must have a head called *Baálé* (father of the house). They do not sit down to elect or select the *Baálé*. He emerges immediately an incumbent dies. The oldest, irrespective of his origin, assumes the position automatically and his recognition is also automatic. It is the same way families have their heads - *Olórí ẹbí*. A stranger today could be so integrated that generations after may have one of his descendants as *baálé*.

The situation above is that of an urban area. If we move to the country side every village is characteristic of a compound in the town. In days gone by village compounds were circular to some extent and were mostly huts and one had to bend the neck or the whole body to enter through the low doorway. Today, buildings in many villages are as standard as those in the urban areas. The houses are more individualistic as in the town, despite the close relationship existing among the villagers.

The *Baálé* is the head of all the people that make up the enclave. He is not a title holder in the town's traditional rulership but his authority is not in doubt in his family. However in Ibadan a *Baálé* known as Mọgaji could become the *Olúbádàn* if he rises in rank to be the most senior chief at the death of the incumbent *Olúbádàn*. This is discussed in full later.

Baálẹ̀

The *Baálẹ̀* is the chief of a village, town or a section of a big town or city. Literally, *Baálẹ̀* means the father or chief owner of the land area like the old English squire. Land there refers to the extent of his domain. Thus, there are many houses or compounds, including villages under his jurisdiction. He controls a large population. *Baálẹ̀* is a title holder under the *Oba* who is the paramount ruler. The number of *Baálẹ̀s* (family or house heads) under him depends on the expanse of his community. Though all land belongs to the *Oba*, the *Baálẹ̀* is the custodian on his behalf. Nobody can own land without the authority of the *Baálẹ̀*. He is nearer to the people than the *Oba*.

The Ọba

The *Ọba* or the King is the paramount ruler in any community in Yoruba land. In the past whatever the *Ọba* said was law and had to be obeyed. In former times very old men ascended the throne of Ọbaship. Nobody could see the face of the *Ọba* which was always covered with beaded tassles woven round his crown. When he talked another person acted as his megaphone. When he greeted his subjects he spoke with a hardly audible tone for his human megaphone to echo *Oba ń kí yín* (the king greets you). *Oba ni e maa rora* (the king welcomes you). If any subject committed an offence the *Oba* could fine him or even banish him, depending on the gravity of the offence. When he fines the offender it means *Oba ta a l'oji*. Young educated men are now *Oba* in their domains. The *Baálè* is appointed and installed with the *Oba's* authority.

Regency

Since the former times till date the situation of regency exists in some Yoruba communities. A young girl under the age of puberty is made to sit on the throne of the *Oba* pending the installation of a new one, that is, after the demise of the incumbent. The interregnum is usually long and acrimonious for contenders. It is when the *Igbimò afòbaje* (the kingmakers) sit on the nominations from contending or contesting families that one person is picked. The person picked will have to be approved by the state governor before installation takes place. It is then that the regent will vacate for the new *Oba*.

Oba-in-Council

Even when the *Oba* was the alpha and omega of the society he did not adjudicate single-handedly but in consultation with certain categories of community chieftains. The council is made up of three categories of citizens. One set is the sectional chiefs, the *Baálè*. The second set is the *Oba's* court advisers such as *Òtún, Òsi, Èèkerin, Asípa* and others, varying in name from place to place. The third set is chiefs of traditional religious bodies. Such bodies include *Orò* (no English equivalent), *Eégún* (masquarade) and cults, but lately christians and moslem chiefs are installed for the *Oba's* court in some Yoruba communities. All the chiefs in the *Oba's* council are hereditary. At given periods either in a day or week they must sit round the *Oba* to consider important issues.

The council bears different names in different places, like *Òyómèsi* for the *Aláàfin* of *Òyó* and *Òsugbo* or *Ògbóni* in *Ègbá* and *Ìjèbú* areas. But there is a common name. It is *Ìlú. Ìlú* means town or city or megacity. Whatever instruction is ascribed to *Ìlú* it is not merely binding but also unalterable. It has become like the ancient law of Meades and Persians.

It is noteworthy that since ancient times till date the Yoruba tradition gives recognition to the role of women in the society. This is why every *Oba* has a woman titled *Ìyálóde* as one of his central chiefs. Her position is not hereditary but by social standing, yet it's a life long title, she must be present at all *Ìlú* meetings.

68

Qualification for Ọbaship

Except in modern times when Ọbaship has become government bonus in certain areas, it used to be restricted to those who were entitled to it because they were of royal blood.

The largeness of a town or city does not qualify it to be ruled by an *Ọba*. Once the head of a town has no ancestral trace to any of the seven children of Oduduwa, the founder of the Yoruba race, or Ile Ife, the ancestral headquarters, he cannot reign or rule with a crown. Not all the seven Oduduwa descendants are within the Yoruba land in Nigeria today. Those within include the *Aláàfin* of Oyo in Oyo State, *Aláké* of Egbaland in Ogun State, *Owá-Bòkun* of Ijeshaland and *Ọràngún* of *Ìlá* in Osun State. One of them, the Ọba of Benin is in Edo State while the other two are enclaved in French speaking Benin Republic. They are *Alákétu* of Ketu and *Onípópó* of Popo. That reminds one of how widely spread the Oyo empire was before the balkanisation of Africa in the 1700's by the European colonialists.

Thus, to be qualified to be crowned *Ọba* of a town one must come from a royal family. Only one family in a town wears a crown; but that family may get many branches as to the number of male children. The number of male children of the first *Ọba* determines the number of branches there may be in a royal family. As the families expand in number the problem of choosing a successor becomes compounded and acrimonious. But what modern government now does for them is to publish a chieftaincy declaration. To arrive at such an instrument a high powered tribunal, headed by an experienced High Court judge is constituted to talk with all princes and others to determine who should and who should not. This system today eases up agitations for the *Ọba*'s stool.

Respect Among *Ọba's* Group

Today, the shaking of hands and hugging are applied when a number of *Obas* come together at a social function. In the past it was not like that. If there were a number of them in a gathering each of them knew his ranking, that is, those who were his seniors traditionally and those junior to him. Since an *Ọba* must not prostrate for anybody, the junior Ọba would simply say with his own mouth that *Mosàapẹ* (he worshipped the senior one) and that's all. If they were seated the junior *Ọba* would send a member of his train to the senior one that he was greeting him with respect. Again, it is a taboo for an *Ọba* to prostrate. Before his coronation he could prostrate but after that he must never again prostrate for any living being. When a group of *Obas* come together they give absolute respect to each other. Generally speaking, the Yoruba cherish their *Ọba's*.

69

Ọba's power

Traditionally, the installation of the Ọba is embedded in deep fetishism of Yoruba occultism. That is how he becomes the father of 'all'. The 'all' there is very broad. Before the advent of Christianity and Islam the Yoruba people were idol worshippers. They worshipped anything like the Biblical Ephesians. Then, the number of idols being worshipped in a town or community depended on how exposed the people were to the outside world. The Ọba must be endowed with all the occultic powers available in all the idols in his domain. This is because nobody else must possess any spiritual power superior to the Ọba's. And the people were so faithful in whatever they did that nothing would be witheld from the Ọba that he really deserved. He was the earthly head of practitioners of witchcraft and sorcery and other esoteric sciences and crafts. The Ọba's diviner was the priest of Ifá Oracle. (Ifá is an oracular practice or object applied in divination).

With the advent of Christianity and Islam the rate of idol worship has been reduced drastically but not eradicated. Thus, the Ọba also becomes the head of Christians and Moslems in his domain. It has already been stated that he is supposed to be the spiritual head of every individual in his domain. This is why he earns the eulogy of Aláse ekeji Òrisà. That is 'the wielder of authority, the second in command to Almighty God'. The ancient Ọba wielded immense and limitless powers. Modern governance has however deprived him of the second only-to-the-Almighty powers. Yet, he is still influential among his subjects.

It is interesting to note that personalities exercising political power today also give great respect to the Ọba. That could be the chairman of the local government where the Ọba reigns or the State Government or even the nation's President. This mutual respect is often shown when those political heads pay courtesy visits to certain grades of Ọbas. Thus, as the Ọba demands certain rights and privileges from the nation's political authorities so do the latter in return require the Ọba to assist the government in reaching the grassroots. The Ọba is the leader at the grassroots like the Baálè.

Ọba's Insignia

The feature for honour of the Ọba does not end in the crown and the sceptre. His throne (seat) in the palace and in public functions, the volume of his robes as well as the train of officials milling round him, together with the heralding music are parts of the bundle of honour trailing the Ọba anywhere he goes .

In practice, no Ọba wears the crown every time, especially in those days when it used to be a heavy object - a crippling load on the neck! The original crown was purely mystical and was worn only on special occasions. Even today when the crown is designed in beads and is much lighter in weight, it is not an every-time cap. But one important thing is that it is forbidden for an *Ọba* to leave his head bare. His head which must be shaved clean to total baldness must always be capped and protected. Nobody must see the skin of his head from the day of his installation. This is why, even the Christian *Ọba* wears a small cap in church.

Another feature for which an *Ọba* is noted is the use of beads - worn as bangles and necklaces. Incidentally, this feature is not only for the *Ọba* but also for his chiefs, as an official insignia and sign for respect. The Ọba controls indigenous music in his domain. By this is meant that wherever talking drums are being beaten and wind instruments bellowed, the praise names and eulogies of the *Ọba* are the first that must come out from there at every occasion or performance. Indigenous singers will start the performance with a salute to the *Ọba*. Once the drummer is within the domain of the *Ọba* the uncoded rule prevails.

It is worthy to note that all drummers and indigenous merry makers, including minstrels know the praise names of all *Ọbas* in Yorubaland as well as those of other individuals since every individual originates from one of a known number of family roots. It is part of their training and unwritten code.

The Ibadan Example

Ibadan, the capital of Oyo State is the largest indigenous city in West Africa. Because of its founding status as a nodal city, it was populated from different places till it has grown to its present size. As a Yoruba community, its governance is not different from what has been said. But, since it did not originally have a link with any Yoruba ancestral royalty it throws its door of paramount headship open to every descendant of the houses or family compounds in the upcoming megacity. In other words, anybody who heads a house as *Mogaji* in any part of the city has the chance to become the *Olúbàdàn* of Ibadan. This is opposed to the practice whereby Ọbaship changed hands among royal families.

In Ibadan, it moves round as to seniority in the membership of *Olúbàdàn* Council. That means, the most senior chief becomes *Ọba* at the death of *Olúbàdàn*. In fact, there have been cases where incumbents died under five years of reign because of old age.

71

Two things are apparent. There are no permanent royal houses and there are no hereditary princes or rather, there are princes or princesses who may never wear the crown unless they head their houses and are lucky to be alive and are senior in the *Olúbàdàn* Council when an incumbent *Olúbàdàn* dies. Thus, succession to the stool of *Olúbàdàn* is unique and peculiar to the Ibadan people alone.

Chieftancy Titles

Chiefs are members of the court of the *Oba* or members of the Oba-in-council, depending on the adopted nomenclatures. As stated earlier, there are three types of chiefs around the *Oba*. Two of them are traditional while the other type is honorary. What we are concerned with here is the honorary chieftancy titles which are often awarded to people who do not belong to any royal family or who are not members of the families of traditional chieftains. Because of the honorary nature, such title holders do not contribute to the day-to-day administration of the community nor do they qualify to advise the *Oba* in such regard. One could liken honorary chieftaincy titles to those given out to both Britons and non-Britons by the British monarch.

In determining who qualifies for the title, factors for consideration are not too deep. It may be given to people who are involved in philanthropic activities; people who initiate projects that are beneficial to the community; those known to have succeeded in their trade over the years; and those who the *Oba* considers to be an asset to the society in one way or the other. Because of such considerations, nativity has no place in it as both indigenes and non-indigenes, including foreigners can qualify for the award. The reason why the award is not the exclusive preserve of indigenes of a community is that non-indigenes and foreigners may perform good deeds in their community of domicile that attract the attention of the *Oba*. The *Oba* then finds an appropriate title by which the work of the holder can be described. For example, if he is a successful trader he could be given the title of *Babalájé* or *Ògbéni Ojà*. If he is an experienced journalist he could be *Onigègé-ara* or *Báàròyin*, for an educationist it could be *Bàbá-imò* or *Olú-imò*, etc. If it is a female socialite she could bag *Ìyá-oge*.

Sometimes, recipients are not given titles according to their profession or performance but by certain seeming or real traditional titles which are already obsolete in the present time. An example of this is *Àare-Ònàkakanfò*. It was given to real war leaders in the old Oyo empire. The title is equivalent to that of a field marshal, a generalissimo. *Balogun* is a war title for any community. It was given to men of valour during the medieval wars. It was a junior

72

position to *Àarẹ̀-ònàkakanfò*. But today, *Balógun* is also used as an antecedent for an array of honorary titles. Ready examples are *Balógun Onígbàgbọ́* (head of Christians) and *Balógun Mùsùlùmí* (head of Moslems) ,etc.

As honorary titleship grows and gets more popular among the citizens, the people's desire for it becomes so high that many no longer wish to be addressed merely as Mister (Mr). This is true of socialites and the *nouveau riche*. At the highest point of insolence, some of these *nouveau riche* even see being described as mere chiefs as *infra dig*, so they go for titles like *Àarẹ*, High Chief, *Ọ̀túnba* or even *Balógun*. Nobody sees anything wrong in this since the holders do not influence the *Ọba* in his administration, particularly since the *Ọba* himself only reigns but does not actually rule.

There are special cases where honorary chiefs do assist the *Ọba* in his administratiion. One example was the case at *Èrùwà* in Oyo State when *Bọ́lánlé Ọláníyan*, the *Gbajúmàla* the second was the *Eleruwa* from 1975 - 1993. He often took counsel for adjudication from one of his honorary chiefs alongside his illiterate traditional chiefs. In some other communities certain honorary chiefs are somehow co-opted into the *Ọba*'s council for advice on critical issues. However, such a position will never make their title become hereditary or traditional as the honour given to them is exclusively personal to them.

The *Ọba* and Religion

The *Ọba* has no religion. What that means is that he belongs to all religions. This is comparable to a nation that practises secularity - not leaning towards any particular religion. The *Ọba* recognises all religions. Even if he attends church or goes to the mosque he must also open himself to the religion of others. Thus, when practitioners of all religions celebrate their faiths or perform their rituals they must intimate the *Ọba* of their celebrations.

Traditionally, the Yoruba *Ọba* is involved in fetishism. There are very many rites he must perform at given periods of time during the year. In fact, once on the throne he immediately throws overboard, at least, two of the Biblical and Quranic commandments against idol worshipping and having another god beside the Almighty God. Despite that, however, many of them still go to church or attend jumat services as christians or moslems.

Chapter 10

Parole

Introduction

The average Yoruba man does not compromise morality for anything. He can go to any length to achieve and maintain it, be it by force or by persuasion. If his grown-up child has some bad behavioural trait he would ask trusted neighbours or family members or even the head of his religious body to counsel him to change for the better. The use of force, including corporal punishment and serious scolding are frequently resorted to in every family to curb the excesses of a ward or child. The persuasion method which greatly influences the mind is today no longer as popular as it used to be under the village or grassroots setting. It is one of the casualties of urbanisation and the so-called modern living - a living standard that attempts to erode the society of such cultural practices that are capable of promoting sound moral standards, without which the society lives in fear of social upheavals. This so-called modern living is mere cultural hybridity resulting from a graft of misdeeds of the West into African life. Parole is applied here as a term to describe the idea and practice of telling moral-building stories or changing bad behaviour by using stories. Most television and radio stations in Nigeria today broadcast programmes that promote morality.

Story telling takes place at nights but usually, informally. In parole, two mammals are often used as principal characters. The first one is a human being called *Ọ̀pálábà* - an all-wise man said to have lived during the early history of the Yoruba. He was an encyclopedia of wisdom, wit and knowledge. The other one, an animal, *Alábáun* or *Ìjàpá* (tortoise) is a cunning animal. He is always a villain. Stories told around *Ọ̀pálábà* are meant to teach people good virtues. Those told around *Ìjàpá* are to show how bad or evil deeds can lead one to shame and disaster. In Yoruba land very many proverbs and wise sayings are sourced from *Ọ̀pálábà*. It is he who lays an example for wise expressions. Thus, his sayings and wise ideas are always applied positively to teach morals.

In the case of *Ìjàpá*, we see an animal not merely cunning but often unsuccessful in his ways for being self-opinionated and unco-operative with others. If stories said to have been told by or told about these two characters are coded, the collections will fill up vast library buildings in every community. Unfortunately, the people then did not have the opportunity of the art of modern writing by which ideas could be stored in written form. It is in this area that the old Greeks are greater than the Yoruba, a people rich in different branches of arts, literature, anthropology, occultism, etc.

Two types of people engage in the story telling business. The first is the parent - the father or the mother. He or she does so either while the food is still cooking or while the family is resting after supper, waiting to go to bed. He or she invites all the children in the home including the wards for the session. It is always interesting and children hate missing it.

The second type of story telling is the one told by a renowned village story teller. While nobody formally confers such an accolade or title on him, everybody, the young and the old alike swarm around him for story sessions most nights. Incidentally, the art of story telling is a natural gift as the narrators never acquire the art formally under the tulelage of a master. The traditional rural setting permitted this. The society today is deprived of parole,especially in urban areas. Even in the rural communities, the urban life that has ebbed there has negatively influenced the values of the people.

Moral reforms are better introduced through parole which is a sort of subtle indoctrination. It is more effective than legislation which moulds society though harshly. Thus, parole system quietly drives the message into the bloodstream of the citizen (listener) thereby turning the subject matter into culture or that which must be attained. Any breach of the act does not land one in the law court via police arrest but brings the culprit to public ridicule in the presence of as many others as may be aware of the misdeed. That is the people's court. In other words, every citizen is a policeman dragging offenders of custom to the justice of public ridicule and condemnation. The fact that breach of custom practices puts the offender to shame makes it easier for parole to reform the society better than the judicial punishment which often times makes hardened criminals of innocent youths, who break the law, and land themselves in the hands of harsh law enforcement officers. That in itself is tantamount to worsening what is already bad, or calling for reform. However, all moral stories always paint God as the rewarder of man according to one's bad or good behaviour. Most stories centre around retributive justice or the law of cause and effect. They are meant to discourage the virtuous

75

from engaging in evil practices. They similarly warn people with bad behaviour to change to good or face the natural consequences.

Parole Pattern

Let us examine in outline the pattern which parole stories take:

(1)   **Ọpálábá on diplomacy**

Ọpálábá was a farmer. He was very generous and so famous that he did not like to offend anybody. Very often when he was going to his farm many villagers would ask him to bring one thing or the other for them on his way back. What he was asked to bring from farm for them included a given number of yam and cassava tubers, ears of corn, some firewood, pumpkins, etc. Ọpálábá would carry a heavy load of these items on his head and shoulders every evening. He would not be able to bring anything for his own wife for domestic use. This became a source of annoyance to his wife because his family had to sleep on empty stomachs for many nights simply because her husband must satisfy other people's quests first. Incidentally, the beneficiaries of the items would turn round to blame Ọpálábá for not caring for his family. Ọpálábá saw reason with his wife after a long time. He decided never to fight or quarrel with anybody but apply the method of tactical disobedence. So, whenever he was going to the farm and people asked him to bring this or that for them on his way back in the evening, Ọpálábá would agree. But in the evening when they demanded for what he was asked to bring for them he would simply and kindly express regret that he forgot that day but would try the next day. He would beg them politely and the people would not quarrel with him. Thus, he adopted this method of polite refusal or tactical disobedience and no longer had to strain his neck carrying heavy loads every evening. He became happier, his family was also happy while his usual neighbours no longer asked him to perform stupid assignment for them. Yet nobody begrudged him. He learned to make himself and his family happy first before thinking of other people's need.

(2)   **The stupid wise man**

Ìjàpá (tortoise personified) is known for outplaying, cheating or debasing whoever that associates with him. One day he decided to store all the wisdom available on earth from every other creature for his own exclusive use. He gathered some in a gourd and was going to hang it at

76

the top of the tallest tree. He slung the gourd round his neck but instead of making it hang at his back he dangled it on his chest, ready to climb the tree. As *Ìjàpá* tried to climb the tree the gourd encumbered him and he fell from the tree stem. He repeated his failure for several hours. People passing by saw him and made jest of him before going away. *Ìjàpá* made the fruitless attempt several times and by the evening a man who was passing by asked him what he was doing. He related his mission and the man told him to sling the gourd behind him. *Ìjàpá* did so and thus found climbing easy. Then he realised that it was foolish of one person to think he could be wiser than the whole world. He found out that sharing wisdom makes a wise man wiser.

(3) Other characters

Apart from the wise messages of *Ọ̀pálábá* and the cunning, self-wise nature of *Ìjàpá* there are other characters around whom parole stories are built. These other characters could be fictitious couples, friends, master and servant, king and subjects, communities or even God and man. Stories told around these characters and a host of others are endless.

Let us see the outlines of some of such stories:

(a) **Couples** - It could be the story of a wicked woman attempting to poison her husband only to meet her own doom or that of a bad husband brutalising his wife only to be punished later in life by his own child. Since the Yoruba believe and practise polygamy, the story could be that of an intolerant wife of a three-wived man who gets shamed in the end. The Yoruba want wives of the same husband to be tolerant of each other. There is the story of a woman in a polygamous home trying to poison the child of her co-wife only to end up mistakingly killing her own child instead. She publicly confessed what really happened.

(b) **Friends** - It could be that of a treacherous friend meeting his doom or a cheated friend getting over it at the expense of the one who cheated him.

There is the story of three greedy friends who tried to play each other out over a sum of money they found and in the end they all died without any of them possessing any of the money.

The telling of moral stories has always been a leisure affair. That means it is rare to see people live by it. Paroling was an informal school for good citizenship.

A Story-Teller

It is unfortunate that the only woman who made story telling a profitable business was Chief (Mrs) Olúrẹ̀mí Ọ̀násányà who died in 1994 at the age of seventy years. She reeled out her first series of stories over the defunct Redifusion in the former Western Region of Nigeria in the 1950's when her stories would cause people to swarm around redifusion boxes wherever they were available. It used to be aired at eight o'clock on Saturday morning. She was doing it for the then Nigerian Broadcasting Service.

The signature tune which became her popular name was *Ọmọ Obòkun Nki yín o. Ọmọ Obòkun* is the description for someone who hails from Ijeshaland with Ilesha as headquarters. So, the signature tune literally means 'greetings from the one from Ijeshaland'. It is an ethnic identity. Mrs Onasanya later moved to Radio Lagos as an artiste at its inception in 1978 and retired from there in the mid eighties. She even had two record albums on moral stories to her credit. Up to 2004 (when this book was published) there has been no replacement to her in parole story telling.

Parole in Music

Different Yoruba musicians include parole stories in a few of their musical works. An example is the popular *Kẹ́tẹ́kẹ́tẹ́* by Ebenezer Obey (real name: Ebenezer Fabiyi). *Kẹ́tẹ́kẹ́tẹ́* means the ass. The story is that nobody can please everybody. Whatever you do somebody will criticise you. It is left for you to do good and stand by it. Similarly, Sunny Ade (real name: Sunday Adegeye) also has his. Those two musicians played *juju* but those playing *Àpàlà* or *Sàkàrà* music are basically parole blazers. They include Aruna Ìshọ̀lá, Yùsúf Olátúnji (alias *Bàbá L 'ẹ́gbà*), *Òjíndò, Nósírù Àtúnwon*, etc. Ballad musicians (*ewi, Ìjálá,* etc.) also thrive in parole pieces. Such musicians include Foyánmu and Ọlátúbọ̀sún Ọládápọ̀. In the case of Félá Aníkúlápó Kúti with his Afrobeat, his parole in pidgin English was directed mainly at the authorities. Generally, indigenous and traditional Yoruba entertainers are moralists.

Chapter 11

Taboos and Superstitions

Introduction

An average Yoruba person is superstitious. This may be due to his absolute belief in God, by whatever means he worships God, and his belief in retributive judgment. There are different superstitions for different facets of life and these can vary from place to place or even to families. Some superstitions are merely meant to enforce either moral or health laws or otherwise to instil discipline. What one could regard as real or serious superstitions are quickly dying out under the scourge of christianity which dismisses superstitions as instruments of negative or satanic forces. All sorts of superstitions are called èèwọ̀, meaning what must not be done or taboo abscention.

There are a number of èèwọ̀ for a woman to observe after child birth. For example, in some families the woman must first eat the meat of a lizard before eating normal meat. She has a maximum of seven days to observe the taboo before the naming ceremony of her baby. In some other families the new mother must not take salt in her food for five or seven days. This is called atọ - lack of salt. There are uncountable other taboos for mothers of new babies, all varying as to families, but the question could be asked why such punitive measures are imposed on mothers at the period of their delicate health condition, immediately after child birth.

Let us use one example to explain the general origin of taboos. There is the story of a slave girl who lived with a family from her youth till she got married into the family of her service. In fact, she had been accustomed to the life and culture of her domiciled community. But because of her background she was hated by rival wives of the same husband. The other women hated the idea of a slave having an offspring to compete with their own children in future whenever family benefits would be shared among them. It was customary for the people to hide certain property or goods in the ceiling of the house for safe keeping. It happened that when this slave wife was in labour one of the senior wives asked her to climb up and bring

79

down something from the dirty ceiling. As soon as she climbed the ladder and go into the ceiling the cruel senior wife removed the ladder, leaving the slave wife travailing in child birth helplesssly in the ceiling. She safely delivered the baby unaided in the ceiling but she died later. Before she died she made the prononcement of the last words of a dying person that henceforth any woman in that family wishing to have safe delivery must first climb to the ceiling on the day of delivery. Any woman who failed to do so would die during child birth. And the pronuncement was obeyed thereafter because of the condition that warranted its issuance.

That example shows that every taboo relating to child birth has something to do with some vengence placed by somebody wrongfully punished for the subject matter of the taboo.

In a village called Aaya near Èrúwà in Oyo State of Nigeria, a girl (in the 1940's) was living as a maid with a notorious tyrannical woman. This girl told her mistress that in her family they do not eat a meal of guinea-corn (c̣ko bàbá). She was about sixteen years old then, and she had never eaten it nor could she say what the result would be if she did. One day her mistress forced her to eat a meal of guinea-corn contrary to the girl's family taboo. After eating the forbidden meal the maid immediately developed goose-flesh all over her face and body and became feverish. Henceforth, she was not forced to eat her family's forbidden meal.

In today's thinking and with the advent of 'civilisation' these types of taboos have become negative to christian ideals. In fact, even in the rural communities most people do not obey such taboos any more .

Some taboos have fetish tendencies. Strictly fetish taboos do exist and they have to do with particular idol or goddess worship. They are not discussed here because the Yoruba traditional religion would be better discussed outside this book.

Abstinence Taboos or Èèwọ̀

Yoruba people approach moral moulding education at different fronts for the purpose of having peaceful homes and society. This is aimed at rearing obedient children in homes where they will eventually grow up to be law-abiding citizens. The method they adopt is to enact different societal ordinances to guard and guide all facets of daily life. These are the taboos of 'don't do' Each of the ordinances is regarded as clauses that must not be infringed upon else there will be immediate or eventual negative consequences. They are the èèwọ̀. Again, these ordinances guide the day-to-day life of the people. It is

80

interesting to note that the abstinence taboos achieve the desired effects as they create fear in the minds of youths towards whom they are apparently directed. So, before the youth realises that there is nothing to fear in the 'don't taboos', his life would have already been moulded in the way his parents and the society want it

Let us consider some of the societal ordinances or the don't taboos.

(1) **Sitting on doorway**: Children are fond of sitting on the doorway either as a daily habit or to express defiance to their particular parent for making them cry. In order to check this act they are told that it is forbidden for a child to sit on the doorway else his mother dies. But children love their mothers very dearly! The nuisance in sitting on doorway is that the passage is either prevented or made difficult. This taboo is thus aimed at preventing such nuisance. Mothers know how to enforce such ordinances to convince their children of the gravity of their offence. If another child threatens to 'tell mummy' the culprit will hurriedly stand up and change his sitting position.

(2) **Spitting indiscriminately**: In order to prevent this in children they are told that it causes sore-throat and bald head. This 'don't' prevents the youth from spitting around the sitting room or just anywhere around the house. He fears contracting a sore throat which may prevent him from eating.

(3) **Talking while eating:** Either or two of these things may likely happen if someone talks while eating: There is the possible health hazard of choking and\ or it would be a nuisance if one should splutter on the face of colleague at meal time. To prevent an occurrence of any of those situations youths are ruled out of talking at meals. This is to check nuisance aspect of it.

(4) **Meat eating at meal times:** Infants are instructed that it is forbidden for them to eat their meat while still eating the main food. They are told to eat the meat after the main food has been eaten. The reason for this is that kids often like to rush whatever they do and thus consume the whole meat of the family for a meal if they have free a hand. What parents do is to share out the meat and place everybody's share in the plate in front of him. Alternatively, the child's share is placed in his left palm and he is asked to close the palm till the end of the meal. If he attempts to eat his meat like others the parent with the appropriate countenance will quickly warn: 'Little children don't eat meat while still eating'.

(5) **Throwing away handwashing water :** Hand washing water is treated as the last topic in chapter four of this book to the degree relevant to that chapter. It gets murky and oily - no matter the type of oil used for the soup. If it is not thrown away quickly the resultant sediment is nauseating while the oily scum also produces a disgustful sight. The normal thing is that after a meal the youngest among the eaters throws away the water. He is told to throw away the handwashing water as it is a taboo to allow it to settle.

(6) **Tooth picking:** They say it is forbidden for children to pick their teeth after a meal. One of the reasons being to discourage them from forming a bad habit. There are many adults who move their tongues within their mouths and behind the teeth to make hissing sounds after meal as if they are whistling. Thus, even when they drink water that habit has been so created that the teeth need picking and since there is no solid foreign body within the teeth that hizzing sound will be made as often as possible. Youths can also damage the gums of their teeth with the toothpick.

(7) **Teeth cleaning and breakfast:** A child who wants to take his breakfast before cleaning his teeth is told it is forbidden. This is simply a hygiene 'don't'.

(8) **Gathering refuse with bare hands:** A child who wants to do so is told that he must not use his bare hands to gather and dispose of refuse, else, his hands will shake uncontrollably. He fears and obeys. This is another sanitation 'don't'.

(9) **Sitting with stretched legs:** A child is not permitted to sit down and spread his legs where adults are passing. The same applies to adults. There are two reasons for this. The first is to stop that child from constituting a nuisance while the second is superstition. It is believed that if a pregnant woman steps on or walks across outspread legs there is a possibility she will bear a child that resembles that person. A pregnant woman would want to step across her husband's legs to have her child in the likeness of him. It actually happens in many cases. People often call on owners of out-stretched legs to remove them so that they can pass.

(10) **Nail cutting:** There are two 'don'ts' on nail cutting. 'Don't cut your nails on the floor'. This is for sanitation. The second one is against cutting the nails at night. This is said to be forbidden, but it is aimed at preventing cutting oneself with a blade at night. It is to prevent personal accidents.

(11) **Dipping mouth into drink/water:** In the original traditional set up, Yoruba people do not drink water from a cup, or a white man's vessel, but from a big container, usually a thoroughly cleaned calabash and more recently, a sizeable dish. The whole family drinks from the same source at meal time. Normally, everybody drinks through the tip of the container but the young child will like to put in his whole mouth into the bowl, smeared with food and probably mucous. The taboo on that is aimed at cleanliness and against being a nuisance- not even against contamination.

(12) **The left hand:** This affects both the child and the adult. It is regarded as a bad habit to use the left hand to give something to another person. An adult can do so. The taboo affects a child more because he has not known that the left hand is different from the right hand. Because of this custom it is almost impossible for children who are born ambidextrous to remain so till adulthood as parents often try to discourage them, at times unsuccessfully and sometimes successfully. There are instances where the youth abandons ampidexterity as a result of parental pressure. The major reason for this taboo is that it is the left hand that is used for cleaning of the anus after toilet, etc. How, can one use that same hand to pass anything to anybody? For the reason of hygiene the left hand is not used for eating.

(13) **Passing amidst people:** If an adult meets two or more people on the way he will not pass between them but sideways for it is culturally indecent to do so. In the same vein if a youth, whether known or unknown, passes between two adults they would either scold him seriously or pull him back, calling him names.

The list is inexhaustible!

Chapter 12

Link with Others

God created man to behave as man wherever he may be, no matter the colour of his skin and the shape of his face. There are similarities and likenesses in man found anywhere. Likeness lies in the fact that every man eats, sleeps, talks, walks and works but what he eats, where he goes or sleeps, how he walks or talks, and the type of work he does may just be similar or outrightly different because of where he lives and the colour of his skin.

Thus, culture varies as to peoples and groups of people in the world. Every homogeneous people have their distinct ways of life. Even among a monogeneous group the extent of their spread or distance from centre usually causes a slight change in their way of life. However, there is a likeness in the culture of the same group of people living even far away from each another. But only similarities occur in the cultures of people who are different from each other even if they live close by. One important basic fact in this respect is that, be it similarity or likeness, no set of people learn their culture from another set. They only discover that at their different locations they are doing the same or similar things naturally. That means culture is a natural phenomenon in its original state. However, vogue incursion alters or redefines aspects of culture into human creation. This process makes culture dynamic. Vogue blazers are always influenced by either their inborn art in creating new things or their love for new things - taste, they import cultures of foreign places they visit. The blazers are either musicians, socialites or designers.

The British
The British have two things in common with the Yoruba. The first is the monarchy. Though the withering of colonialism and lately modern government whittled down the authority of the Yoruba *Oba* who used to wield all the powers now being possessed by the government. The second is orderly governance. Before the arrival of the white man there was good system of governance and there was good followership in Yoruba land. Though unlike

the British there has always been multiplicity of *Oba*, but there has always been a paramount ruler to ensure the absence of conflicts in a particular domain.

The Greeks
The Greeks of old were the leaders when we talk of mythology. The richness of the Yoruba in it is not known much largely because Western education and its orthography got to them rather late. Otherwise, Yoruba myths and mythology would surely have been codified and recognised worldwide just like the ancient Greeks..

The Hausa
They have a lot in common culturally with the Yoruba but because we are examining only behavioural culture we shall limit ourselves. In the art of respect the two peoples are similarly linked. There are great similarities in the display and the demand for respect that exists in the two ethnic peoples. Music and dressing are two areas where both similarities and likenesses occur but details of these are outside the scope of this book.

Tribal Marks
There are ethnic groups in the northern parts of Nigeria like the Kànúrí and the Ìgalà whose tribal marks have similarities with sections of the Yoruba people. The Kanuri with long head-to-cheek vertical tribal marks (Gombo) are said to have the same ancestral origin with the Yoruba. The Igala with horizontal marks on their cheeks have similar behaviour with the Yoruba.

The Hebrew
It is uncertain if the sentimental similarities between the Yoruba and the Hebrew of old have ever been examined. The history of the origin of the Yoruba indicates that they came from the Middle East without specifying which side - Jewish or Arabic. We are taught that *Lamurodu* (by Yoruba dialect and orthography) or Nimrod was the father of Oduduwa who founded the Yoruba race. We are not told whether Oduduwa was a direct son of Nimrod or he was distant in the lineage. However, the Christian Bible mentions that Nimrod was a descendant of Noah (Genesis 10:8). If the Yoruba people who were 'stark illiterates' in terms of Western education, could by oral history give an account that tallies with a great written record like the Bible, then the veracity of such a claim should not be in doubt. Nimrod was a hunter (Gen. 10:9). Yoruba ancestors who founded their present settlements were hunters alongside whatever other things they did. One may yet be sceptical about the claim but when we consider a few examples of

biblical account of the life or culture of the old Hebrews side-by-side with the life of the Yoruba, one cannot help but develop the sentiment. The following are a few examples:

(1) **Circumcision** -This may not be peculiar to the Yoruba but common with different races around the globe, especially Africa. It is God's injunction, according to Genesis 17:10-14 and 21:4.

(2) **Entertaining strangers** (Genesis 18:1-8, Exodus 22:21 and Leviticus 19:33, 34). Till today the traditional Yoruba still entreats strangers around them to accept being entertained or hosted to some pleasantries. That is, they are generous to strangers. Their claim is that someone entertaining a stranger would get favour whenever he goes to a foreign environment or his own children may meet benevolent people whenever they are far away from home.

(3) **Husband as lord** (Genesis 18:12) - It is traditional for the Yoruba wife to address her husband as her lord. Those doing so are not in any way influenced by Christianity at all. In the Yoruba context 'lord' means somebody who has sole authority over the other and who also provides all the needs of that other person.

(4) **Dowry** (Genesis 24:53) - This is not in the British context, but the way the old Hebrew did it is the way the Yoruba still do it today, whereby it is the groom who presents gifts to the bride and her parents. Read more in chapter one under marriage.

(5) **Bride's maid** (Genesis 29:24,29) - Traditionally, when a lady is getting married she leaves her parents' home with a maid to assist her in her new home. She does not use the maid as a slave but as a loving help as such maids are usually blood-related to their mistresses.

(6) **Bidding a bride farewell when she is going to her groom's house with parental or traditional prayer** (Genesis 24:60). The prayer is usually led by the head of the larger family. The two parents are included in the family's farewell prayer for the bride or groom which is always said in turns. Each of the parents will first eat three to four grains of alligator pepper with a little bite of kolanut before praying. Today, the use of spirits is tolerated. A certain quantity of the spirit is put into a cup and the oldest man in the family pours a little of it on the ground; the bride or groom touches the spot where the spirit is poured with two fingers and uses the fingers to touch his or her forehead and listens to the prayers. Alternatively, prayer is said into a cup of spirit and given to the bride or groom to sip. She or he will have to sip the spirit after the appropriate people have in turn prayed into it

(7) **The bride and the veil** (Genesis 24: 65). The bride veils her face when going to her groom's home. This could last for one to three weeks, depending on the family. Veiling is probably to shield her face so that people around would not notice that she is weeping as she might be homesick for a few days. She begins to weep immediately her mother starts praying for her. This is a permanent separation from her parents! Veiling is also a mark of shyness. In fact, a new wife must show some shyness to gain respect and dignity in the eyes of the people.

(8) **Child's name depicting situations or events** (Genesis 29: 32,33) New born babies get names depicting the circumstances surrounding their birth. It could be that of joy, sorrow, risk, shame, success, etc.

(9) **Marriage according to seniority** (Genesis 29:26) - The inability of the senior child to secure a suitor in time often delays the marriage of his/her younger siblings. However, when such a delay persists, the younger one could get married before the senior but without any ceremony.

(10) **The practice whereby the next-of-kin of a dead man takes on his widow as wife** (Genesis 38:8) - This is called *isúpó* and is still being practised by the traditional Yoruba. The widow is called *opó*.

(11) **Visitor presenting gift to his host** (Genesis 43:11,12) - This has been treated in chapter 5 of this book.

(12) **Punishment for a burglar** (Exodus 22:2) - It is western civilisation that changed the course of things, and its legal system seems to encourage the multiplicity of crimes. Prior to Western influence, burglars who were caught in the act got capital punishment. The reason is that burglars today kill victims who recognise them. The Biblical punishment is indirectly capital.

(13) There is a kind of loin to knee cloth or knee-breeches that was worn by Yoruba men such as hunters, farmers and youths in the olden days. This type of breeches was one of the items of clothing prescribed by God for his worship as contained in Exodus Chapter 28 verse 42. It is interesting that many elitist youths and vogue blazers today drive their sports cars with knee breeches under multi-colour sports shirts! In fact, the Hausas also put on this type of knickers. It is called *Kán-án-kún* by the Yoruba.

(14) Like the Hebrew people (Leviticus 13:46) lepers in Yoruba land have always lived in huts away from the community.

(15) Tasseled clothes (Numbers 15:37-40) - The Yoruba of old used to wear knee breeches with or without jumpers with tassels all round the bottoms.

(16) The Ondo dialectic group in Yoruba land has a special food called *asùn* as part of the feast during social or family ceremonies. The *asùn* is made from smoked beef. The 'smoke' does not really mean the white or black fume but the meat being made eatable by placing it directly in burning coke. *Súyà* of the Hausa is also prepared in this manner. The Biblical example is found in Deuteromy 16:7.

(17) Yoruba pagans fix their special sacrifice days by three or seven days. Three days is called *ita* while seven days is *ije*. Similar to the latter is what is recorded in Deuteronomy 16:15.

(18) The Yoruba have it that a woman has no religion of her own but adopts that of her husband (Ruth 1:16).

(19) The gregariousness of the Yoruba has been treated. Similarities are many in the Bible. For example, 1samuel 21:1.

(20) **Meeting a guest on his way** (2Kings 4:26) has always been part of Yoruba tradition. If the host cannot do so he will ask somebody else to do it for him, thus leading the visitor into the home. It is done only to visiting friends, equals, seniors and monarchs. This is different from meeting him at the port or bus stop, this is while he is approaching the host's home.

(21) **Like King Ahaz did at a new altar** (2kings 16:13) the Yoruba pagan performs what is called *Ìyánlè* by putting a very tiny portion of the sacrifice (usually food) at a particular spot on the floor before worship prayer is said. Before traditional priests and other adherents taste their meal they first perfom *Ìyánlè* to honour their gods and remember the departed.

(22) **Mourner's bread or cake** (Jeremiah 16:7) - When a senior member of a family dies, a mourner's cake is prepared on the 40th day of his death and distributed randomly to members of the family of the deceased.

(23) **Seeking divination** (Ezekiel 21:21) or **Prophecy** (Judges 18:5 and 1Samuel 30:7,8) as the Kings of the old Hebrew times did so also does the Yoruba *Oba* from time immemorial till date. In the past it was mainly from *Ifá* oracle but today many of them add or prefer prophecy from an *Aládùrá* (Christian) prophets. However, only very few *Obas* seek prophecy openly, it is mostly a nocturnal or 'Nichodemus' affair. The *Ifá* diviner is at the service of every Yoruba *Oba*.

(24) Another of the many examples of cultural similarities between the old Hebrew and the Yoruba is the practice of worshipping with sacrifice. Judiasm, as practised by the old Hebrews was a system of sacrifice and taboos which is almost the same thing as the *baba-láwo* practice of the Yoruba people till today.

(25) **Creation:** It is striking that the traditional Yoruba, through *Ifá* oracle believe and hold that *Olódùmarè* or the Almighty God created the earth. But *Ifá* account of creation started after Noah's ark came on earth after the flood. According to *Ifá* oracle, *Olódùmarè* sent *Òrùmìlà* (a supernatural man) down for the creation. God gave him a special sand to spread on the prevailing water which when he did the earth was formed but it was first in molten form before solidifying. This is why till today the Yoruba describe a gentleman (well behaved person) as *Omolúàbí* or *Omo ti Nóàh bí* meaning the child born of Noah. They often describe man generally as *Omo Ádámù* -meaning the offspring of Adam. This shows their knowledge of Adam.

(26) **Life after death:** The Yoruba strongly believe in life after death which also can be called life in death. Such a belief is in two parts. In the first part, they believe that the dead are not terminally gone but their spirit lurks around. This is why in the traditional setting they celebrate masquerade (*egúngún*) festival annually to remember and appease the spirit of the dead for the comfort of the living. Also in individual traditional families, when the head of an extended family dies they often end their social ceremonies for him with special masquerade outings. At the end of *ìje* (the seventh day of his death) all the children in the extended family will be made to line up by the grave of the deceased while the masquerade prays for them.

In the second part they believe that there is a heaven - a place where the spirits of the dead go. Two expressions, for example, indicate this belief. The first one, *Ayé ni Ojà, òrun ni ilé* means 'the world is a mere market place, heaven is man's home to where he returns after buying and selling'. The second expression is, *Ìgbà mélò ni a ó lò ní ayé tí a nwọ ẹwù irin*. It means that 'life is too short for man to wear clothes made of iron or steel'. Such an expression is often directed against someone who spoils himself with mundane things or who always expresses fear for the unknown.

There are two other expressions touching on the end of good and bad people. When somebody who is known for cruelty, for example, dies, they sort of curse him *À kú tún kú*. That means 'may he die again and again after his physical death'. This suggests a belief in hell. When good people die they pray *òrun rere o*, meaning 'may he go to paradise'. They may also say, *Olórun yóò gbe sí alčlč rcrc o,* meaning 'may God lead him to a spiritual life of bliss' or 'may he live well after death'.

Appendix

Pronunciation Guide
to Most Yoruba Words Used in this Book

The pitch variation and voice modulation of spoken Yoruba language does not exceed 'd' 'r' 'm' when we consider the musical tonic solfa scale. There is no fourth pitch for oral Yoruba except while singing.

The words are arranged in alphabetical order for easy reference while the syllables and the pronunciation guide in solfa notation are enclosed in brackets. Only expressions that do not exceed three words are included. Proverbs and expressions are not included since this is not a language book.

There are seven vowels in Yoruba language as against five in English. These are: a e ẹ i o ọ u. Each sounds like the underlined in the accompanying words in the following: a(far), e(obey), ẹ(pen), i(beat), o(obey), ọ(saw), u(too).

Yoruba language is similar to French in the area of nasal words and their pronunciations. The nasal words end with two letters - a vowel and a terminal 'n' i.e.- an, -en, -in, -on, - un but 'e' and 'o' have no nasal variations. For '-gb-', you just attempt to pronounce the two letters at once. Yoruba equivalence of 'sh' is 'ṣ'.

Aàrẹ	(a-a-rẹ : d d r)
Àáró	(a-a-ro : d m d)
Abàmì	(a-ba-mi : r d d)
Àbíkú	(a-bi-ku : d m m)
Adé	(a-de :r m)
Adéçeyè	(a - de - gẹ - ye : r m r d)
Àjo	(a - jo : d r)
Akolú	(a - kọ - lu : r r m)
Alábaun	(a-la-ba-un :r m r r)
Alárenà	(a- la - re - na : r m r d)
Àlejò	(a- -le- jo : d r d)
Alájọbí	(a- -la - jọ - bi : r m r m)

90

Aláfin	(a - la - a - fin - : r m d r)
Alákétu	(a - la - ke - tu : r m m r)
Àmàlà	(a - ma- la : d d d)
Aníkúlápó	(a - ni - ku - la - po : r m m m m)
Ànkoo	(a- n - ko - o : d d m d)
Àpàlà	(a- pa- la : d d d)
Arúnà	(a - a - ru - na - : r m m d)
Aṣọ	(a - ṣo- : r r)
Atúnnwọn	(a - tun - wọn : r m r)
Awéléwà	(a - wẹ - lẹ - wa : r m m d)
Àwon	(a - wọn : d r)
Baálé mi	(ba- -a - le mi : r m m r)
Baálè	(ba - a - lẹ : r m d)
Baàròyìn	(ba - a- ro - yin : r d d d)
Baba	(ba - ba : r r)
Bàbá alájọ	(ba - ba a -la - jọ : r r r m r)
Babalájọ	(ba - ba - la - jọ : r r m r)
Babaláwo	(ba - ba - la - wo : r r m r)
Balógun	(ba - lo - gun : r m r)
Bólánlé	(bo - la - n - le : m m m m) (n = un)
Dóógó	(do - o - go : m m m)
Eégún	(e - e - gun : r m m)⌒
Egúngún	(e - gun - gun : r m m)
Elérùwà	(e - le - ru - u - wa : r m d m d)
Emèrè	(e - me - re : r d d)
Eré	(e - re : r m)
Èrúwà	(e - ru - wa : d m d)
Èsúsú	(e - su - su : d m m)
Ewì	(e - wi : r d)
Enyín-afè	(e - yin - a - fẹ : r m r m)
Enyín-aró	(e - yin- a - ro : r m r m)
Ẹ	(ẹ : r)
Ẹbí	(ẹ - bi : r m)
Èdá	(ẹ - da : d m)
Ẹgbé	(ẹ - gbẹ : r m)
Ẹgbéjọdá	(ẹ - gbẹ - jọ - da : r m r m)
Ẹgbá	(ẹ - gba : d m)
Ẹgbón	(ẹ - gbọn : d m)
Ẹ káàbọ	(ẹ ka - a - bọ : r m d d)

Èko bàbà	(ẹ - kọ ba - ba : d r d d)
Ẹ kú	(ẹ ku : r m)
Ẹlẹ́dàá	(ẹ - lẹ - da : r m d m)
Ẹ máa kálọ	(ẹ ma - a ka - lọ : r m r m r)
Ẹ pèlẹ́	(e pẹ - lẹ : r d m)
Ẹyin	(ẹ - yin : d r)
Èyọ̀	(ẹ - yọ : d d)
Fábiyi	(fa - bi - yi - i : m m d m)
Felá	(fẹ - la : r m)
Fọ́nyánmu	(fọn - yan - mu : m m r)
Funfun	(fun - fun : r r)
Gèlè	(ge - le : d d)
Gbajúmọ́lá	(gba - ju - mọ - la : r m m m or r m r m)
Ìbàdàn	(i - ba - dan : d d d)
Ìbàdí-àrán	(i - ba - di -a - ran : d d m d m)
Ìbàràpá	(i - ba - ra - pa : d d d m)
Ifã	(i - fa : r m)
Igbóọrà	(i - gbo - ọ - ra : r m r d)
Ìjálá	(i - ja - la : d m m)
Ìjàpá	(i - ja - pa : d d m)
Ìjẹ̀sà	(i - jẹ - sa : d d d)
Ìjokòó	(i - jo - ko -o : d r d m)
Ilé-ifẹ̀	(i - le - i - fẹ : r m r d)
Ilẹ̀-òrẹ́	(i - lẹ - ọ - rẹ : r d d m)
Ìlú	(i - lu : d m)
Ìnáwó	(i - na - wo : d m m)
Ìre	(i - re : d r)
Isẹ̀	(i - sẹ : r m)
Ìsọ̀lá	(i - sọ - la : d d m)
Ìwọ	(i - wọ : d r)
Ìwòran	(i - wo - ran : d d r)
Iwájú	(i - wa - ju : r m m)
Ìyálóde	(i - ya - lo - de : d m m r)
Iyán	(i - yan : r m)
Ìyá - Oge	(i - ya - o - ge : d m r r)
Ìyá ọkọ mi	(i - ya ọ - kọ mi : d m r r r)
Ìyàwó	(i - ya - wo : d d m)
Jòó	(jo- o : d m)
Jòwó	(jọ - wọ : d m)

Kábíyèsí	(ka - bi - ye - si : m m d m)
Lágbájá	(la - gba - ja : m m m)
Láwóre	(la - wo - o - re : m m r r)
Mágùn	(ma - gun : m d)
Mùsùlùmí	(mu - su - lu - mi : d d d m)
N kíi yín	(n ki- -i yin : m m r m) (n =un)
O	(o : r)
Òo	(o - o : d r)
Ó dàbò	(o da - bo : m d d)
O'duà	(o - o - du - a : r d r d)
Óòduà	(o - o - du - a : r d r d)
Odùduwà	(o- du - du - wa : r d m d)
Ògbóni	(o - gbo - ni : d m r)
Ògún	(o - gun : r r)
Òjíndò	(o - ji - n - do : d m d r)
Olójú egé	(o - lo- - ju ẹ - gẹ : r m m r m)
Olójú-oge	(o - lo - ju - o - ge : r m m r r)
Olúbàdàn	(o - lu - ba - dan : rm d d)
Onigbàgbó	(o - ni - gba - gbọ : r m d m)
Onípópó	(o - ni - po - po : r m m m)
Oríkì	(o - ri - ki : r m d)
Orò	(o - ro : rd)
Òsùgbó	(o - ṣu - gbo : d d m)
Òun	(o - un : d r)
Ọba	(ọ - ba : r r)
Ọbàsékú	(ọ - ba - sẹ - ẹ - ku : r r d r m)
Ògá	(ọ - ga : d m)
Ògbéni Ọjà	(ọ - gbẹ - ni ọ - ja : d m r r d)
Òjélàdé	(ọ - jẹ - la - de : d m d m)
Òjòjò	(o- jọ - jọ : d d d)
Ọkọ mi	(ọ - kọ mi : r r r)
Ọládàpò	(ọ - la da - pọ : r m d d)
Ọlátúbòsún	(ọ - la - tu - bọ - sun : r m m d m)
Ọláníyan	(ọ - la - ni - yan :r m m r)
Ọlátúnjí	(ọ - la - tun - ji :r m m m)
Ọlójó	(o- lọ - jọ : r m m)
Ọlórun	(ọ - lọ - run : r m r)
Omobòkun	(ọ - mọ- bo - kun : r r d r)
Ònàkakaǹfò	(ọ - na - ka - ka - n - fo : d d r r d d) (n=un)

93

Ònàsànyá	(ọ - na - a - san - ya ː r d m d d)
Òpálábá	(ọ - pa - la - ba ː d m m d)
Owábòkun	(ọ - wa - bo - kun ː r m d r)
Òwè	(ọ - wè ː d d)
Ọ̀yọ́	(ọ - yọ ː d m)
Ọ̀yọ́mèsì	(ọ - yọ - mi - si ː d m d d)
Pèlé	(pẹ - lẹ - ː d m)
Sàráà	(sa - ra - a ː d m d)
Sárẹ́-pẹgbẹ́	(sa - re - pẹ - gbẹ ː m m r m)
Sàkàrà	(sa - ka - ra ː m m d)
Ṣé kò bù?	(sẹ ko bu? ː m d d)
Wọn	(wọn ː r)
Yakọ mì	(ya-kọ mi ː r r r)

www.ingramcontent.com/pod-product-compliance
Lightning Source LLC
Chambersburg PA
CBHW080427270326
41929CB00018B/3189